CW01572642

Village and Town Life

Sheila Ferguson

Batsford Academic and Educational Ltd London

Typeset by Tek-Art Ltd, London SE20
and printed in Great Britain by
R. J. Acford
Chichester, Sussex
for the publishers
Batsford Academic and Educational Ltd,
an imprint of B.T. Batsford Ltd,
4 Fitzhardinge Street
London W1H 0AH

ISBN 0 7134 4301 4

ACKNOWLEDGMENT

The Author and Publishers would like to
thank the following for their kind permission
to reproduce copyright illustrations:
Aerofilms Ltd, fig 4; Beamish North of
England Open Air Museum, Co. Durham,
fig 60; Birmingham Central Library
(Benjamin Stone Collection), fig 49; BBC
Hulton Picture Library, figs 1, 9, 16, 24, 29,
37, 38, 40, 52, 54, 56, 59, 61; *Cambridge
Evening News*, fig 66; J. Allan Cash Ltd, fig
63; Sue Chapman, figs 64, 65, 67; Dover
Publications, figs 13, 20; Mary Evans Picture
Library, figs 11, 12, 19, 30, 32, 41; Sheila
Ferguson, fig 14; Pat Hodgson Library, figs
2, 5, 6, 7, 8, 10, 15, 17, 23, 25, 28, 33;
Institute of Agricultural History and
Museum of English Rural Life, University of
Reading, fig 46; A. F. Kersting, fig 47;
Mansell Collection Ltd, figs 21, 26, 35, 36,
42, 57, 58; Museum of London, figs 18, 27,
31, 34; Norfolk County Council, fig 45;
Oxfordshire County Council Libraries, figs
43, 44, 53; Ann Ronan Picture Library, fig
39; Warwick Record Office, fig 50. Thanks
are also due to Pat Hodgson for the picture
research on the book.

Contents

The
Illustrations

1
The Middle Ages

The Medieval Village

Much of England in the early Middle Ages was sparsely inhabited and consisted of uncleared forest and vast tracts of unfertile land. Clearings had been made, especially in the centre and south-east of the country, where people worked the land in some nine thousand scattered farming communities. The people lived in hamlets, villages and a few small country towns.

The manorial village originally was the most common type of settlement. Ownership and use of land were laid down in the feudal system developed by William the Conqueror. Under this system the monarch claimed all the land of England for himself, but divided it up among tenants-in-chief (who included great lords, bishops and abbots) in return for their help in running and defending the country and for certain payments. In turn, the tenants-in-chief handed on parcels of land to lesser knights who paid in dues and services, such as providing fighting men when needed. At the bottom of the feudal pyramid were the villeins and serfs. The villeins were allotted plots of land by a lord of the manor in return for services and dues; the services included working on the lord's land and going to fight if called on. The serfs, who were little more than slaves, had no land and worked for their keep.

1 William the Conqueror presenting a charter to his vassal, the Earl of Richmond, setting out the terms under the feudal system by which he held land from the king.

▼

The feudal system tended to create two levels of society in the countryside: land-owners and land-workers — those who commanded and those who obeyed. In the towns there was also a small, independent middle class of merchants, craftsmen and lawyers; and in both town and country there were churchmen of various kinds. The great bulk of the population, however, were villeins and serfs who were tied to the manor where they were born. They were not legally slaves, as they could only be bought and sold along with the land they cultivated. The system gave the village people a certain amount of security, but no personal freedom. The villein and his family could not change their lot in life: they could not leave the village without the lord's consent and even had to get permission to get married. There were also a few free-holders who paid rent to the lord of the manor for their land; they were usually poor and, though not compelled to work on the lord's land, had little more freedom than the villeins.

The typical medieval village consisted of three big open fields divided into long, narrow strips (usually 22 yards by 220 yards) separated from each other by balks of turf. Each man's holding was not in one piece, but scattered through the fields to give everyone a fair share of the good and bad land. Everyone had the right to a share of the meadow land, to keep animals on the common land and to gather fuel in the forest. As there was not enough fodder to feed the animals during the winter, most of them were killed off in the late autumn and salted for the winter. Everyone had to plant and harvest the same crop at the same time. The normal routine was to cultivate only two of the three fields each year while the third was left fallow to recover its fertility. Farming was a mixture of cooperative effort and individual ownership; ploughs and oxen were often shared by groups of villagers, but each man looked after his own strips of land; and his produce — once he had paid in service and dues — was his own.

The manorial system with its open-field villages did not apply to the whole country. To the north and west, where the soil was poorer and the climate cool and wet, the land was more suitable for pasture for sheep, cattle and pigs. Many fields were enclosed and there tended to be isolated farms and small hamlets rather than compact villages.

Many villages were almost self-sufficient. The only essentials needed from outside were salt for preserving and iron for tools and ploughshares, carried round the country on the backs of pedlars or on pack-horses. The grain crops provided the peasant family's main food and drink — bread and ale — and this was supplemented by vegetables, milk and cheese from their cows, and the occasional meat of their animals. It was only a meagre living at the best of times, and if the harvest was poor, starvation was just round the corner. Nearly three-quarters of the peasants had only about fifteen acres of arable land to farm. According to some recent calculations, this would provide a family of five, for instance, in an average year, with one pound of grain per head

2 Villeins harrowing the land and chasing off birds with a sling. From the Luttrell Psalter, 1340.

▼

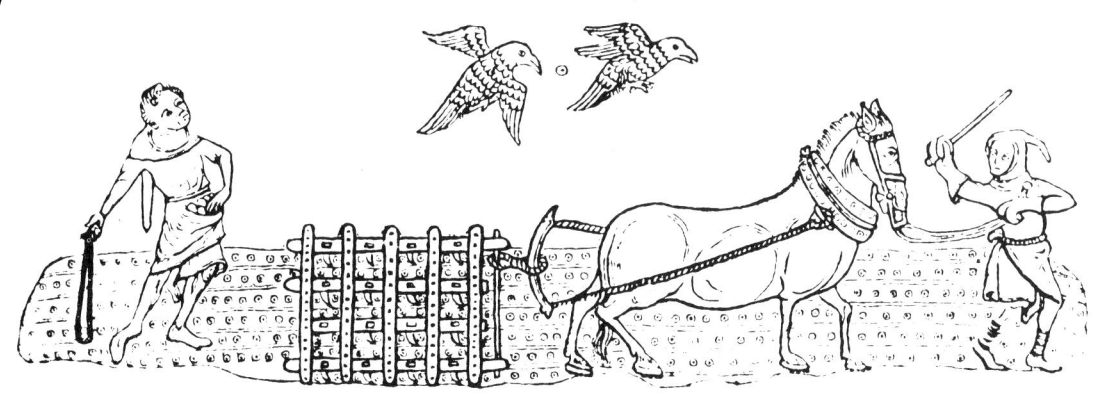

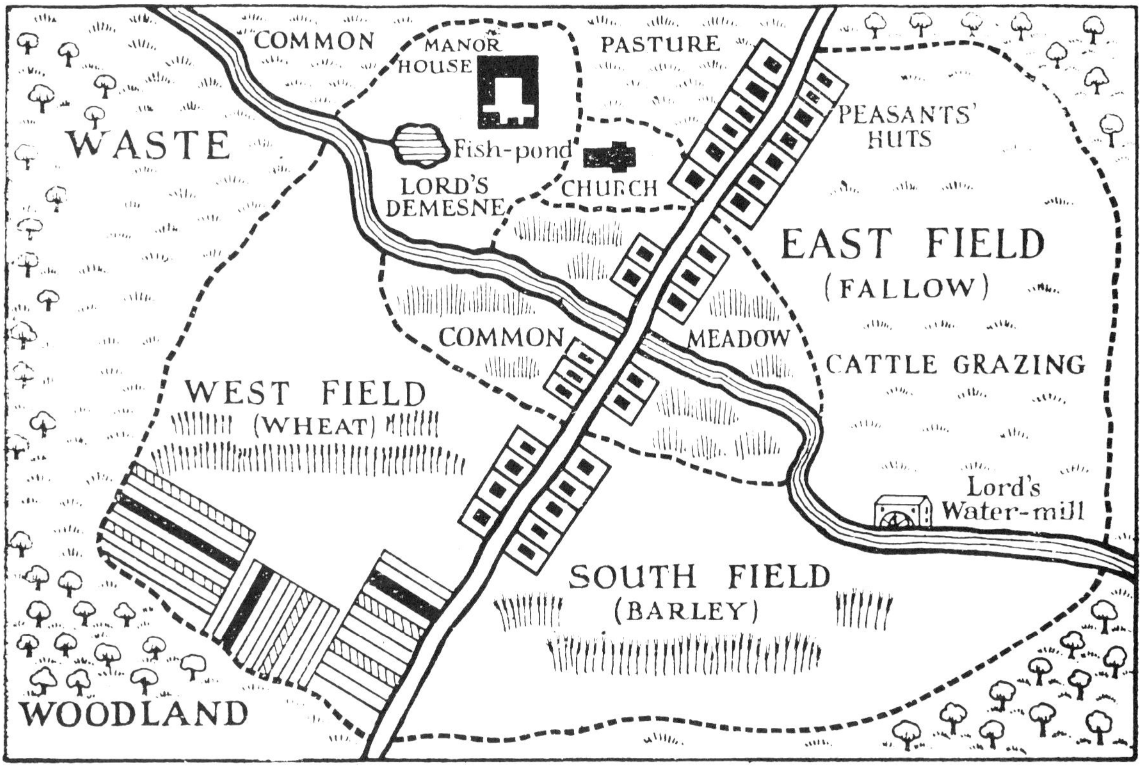

3 Plan of a typical medieval village. Some strips have been marked in in the West Field.

4 Aerial photograph showing the pattern of the old strip-farming at Laxton, Nottinghamshire.

per day. This is below the minimum amount calculated in modern times by the United Nations to keep a family alive, and the estimate was made for an "average" year, whereas perhaps one year in four the harvest failed.

The peasants in the medieval village lived in cottages, which were mere shacks of wattle and daub (wood and mud) set on crofts or small-holdings. The croft was a vegetable plot, space perhaps for poultry and a pig and for tools. The cottage might have only one or possibly two small rooms with mud floors, no windows, and a hole in the roof for the smoke from the hearth to escape. There was very little furniture except perhaps a wooden chest and a stool or two. The people slept on the floor on mattresses stuffed with straw, under home-made woollen blankets. They had few house-hold goods other than iron cauldrons and hand-made wooden plates, bowls and spoons. As well as the simple homes of the villeins and serfs, the typical village would also have a large manor house surrounded by the lord's "demesne", a church, a priest's house with his "glebe" and perhaps houses for a steward, bailiff and a miller.

The villein paid for his cottage, croft and land by working for two or three days a week on the lord of the manor's land, either in the demesne or in the open fields; and by doing extra work at seed time and harvest and paying certain regular dues like two hens at Easter or a pig at Michaelmas. He also had to give the priest, who farmed his own glebe, a tithe (one tenth) of his harvest. Therefore, the villein had little or no surplus produce to sell, though the lord and to a lesser extent the priest would certainly have produce to dispose of at the local market.

Work on the land for the peasant family was hard and heavy, and the hours of labour were long. When darkness fell, the only light in the cottage was the feeble glow given by a rushlight dipped in fat. Clothes were rough and home-made, from wool or leather from the animals. Life was short and uncertain, with death from starvation or the plague always lurking near at hand. The villager was haunted by fears of demons and devils and the fiery pit of hell into which sinners were cast when they died. The

6 Frightening medieval picture of souls in Hell being punished for their sins.
▼

5 The windmill was usually owned by the lord of the manor and the tenants and villeins had to use it and pay him with a fixed percentage of milled flour.
▼

8

7 Mummers who entertained at medieval feasts with singing, dancing and short plays.

priest had great influence over his flock, as he alone could read and interpret the Bible story to them. The parish church was the centre of the poor people's lives — for regular Sunday attendances, weddings, christenings and burial services, the celebration of religious and harvest festivals and sometimes some schooling for the children. The pictures on the walls of the church told the legends of the Christian faith and gave some consolation to the peasant whose life was beset with poverty and squalor.

Apart from church festivals, the main amusements for most villagers were feasts and entertainments provided by the lord of the manor in the Great House at Christmas-time and perhaps open-air feasts run by the villagers to celebrate spring or the harvest. The lord would usually contribute plenty of good food and drink and the gatherings would

be entertained by jugglers, singers and storytellers. There would probably be singing and dancing.

Most village people never in their whole lives travelled more than eight or ten miles from the place where they were born. They had no transport, and the roads were so poor that the most ambitious journey they were likely to make was on foot to the nearest town or to a local fair. In the towns, especially in the ports, people rubbed shoulders with foreign merchants from distant lands and traders from all parts of the country. The world of the townsman was infinitely wider and more varied than that of the countryman.

9

Population and Pressure for Change

Between the count made for Domesday Book in 1086 and about 1300 the population is believed to have doubled and probably reached more than three million. This led to a great hunger for land, as families of the villeins multiplied and fewer strips in the open fields were allotted to each single farmer. The growth of towns increased the demand for food, and manors near towns found a good market for their produce. More waste land was cleared and brought into cultivation.

By the twelfth and thirteenth centuries there were already some changes in the manorial system. Lords of the manor had sometimes been willing to commute (change one sort of payment for another) the forced labour by the villeins on their land for money rents. But as the population grew and land was scarcer, landowners were driving harder bargains. In the middle of the fourteenth century the tide turned again with the disaster of the Black Death (1348-1349). A third or possibly half of the people in the country died of the bubonic plague.

A frightened monk wrote of the repeated deaths he saw and how he expected to die himself. "That pestilence", he wrote,

deprived of human inhabitant villages and cities, and castles and towns, so that there was scarcely found a man to dwell therein; the pestilence was so contagious that whosoever touched the sick or the dead was immediately infected and died; and the penitent and the confessor were carried together to the grave.

The monk said that he was writing his account while awaiting his own death and that he would leave his parchment for any man who survived to continue his work. After listing one more death the handwriting changed and another writer recorded: "Here it seems the author died."

Now, instead of a land shortage, there were not enough labourers to till the soil. Peasants were able to take over neglected strips and even employ hired labour. They were highly reluctant to work on the lord's land and pressed hard to pay rent instead. The landlords found that, with the money they received instead of field service, they could pay wages to labourers without land. The wide gap between the lord and the villein that had been typical of the feudal manor had narrowed. There was now a solid middle class of yeomen farmers and, beneath them, a class of landless labourers. In 1381 the Peasants' Revolt flared up in protest against the remaining villein services and new taxes, and out of fear that the landlords might try to enforce again the old feudal dues and duties.

In the countryside local government in the medieval manor had been in the hands of the lord of the manor and his officials, who based their judgement on local customs. However, in many cases, through the breakdown of feudalism, local control was no longer strong. Therefore, the Crown appointed local gentry to be Justices of the Peace, to govern the neighbourhood in the King's name and to provide the machinery to enforce national policy if required.

The Growth and Independence of Towns

At the time of the Norman invasion there were about a hundred settlements large enough to be called "boroughs" and sixteen boroughs already important enough to be described as cities. Towns such as York, Bristol or Norwich had three to four thousand inhabitants, but London was quite outstanding with nearly 30,000 citizens. Apart from London, all of them had grown out of villages.

There were many reasons why villages grew into towns where they did during the Middle Ages. Firstly, the Norman rulers built many castles from which they could keep order and defend themselves if necessary; the local people in places like Ludlow and Pembroke built houses outside the castle walls, because they felt protected there, and they were able to supply the needs of the garrison for food, other supplies and entertainment. Similarly, the building of monasteries and churches meant that help was provided for the sick, shelter for travellers and opportunities for scholarship; and so religious centres like Canterbury, Durham and Winchester flourished. The expansion of trade, especially the wool trade, was another major reason for the growth of towns. Seaports like Southampton, Hull and Bristol became big and wealthy, and by the fourteenth century when the woollen cloth trade had begun to flourish, towns like Salisbury, Exeter and Colchester were centres of this thriving industry. Other towns, like Oxford and Cambridge with their universities, and Norwich with its silverware, had developed their own specializations and reputation — but London above all had become the acknowledged capital city.

A fair size for most medieval towns was only two or three thousand inhabitants, so they were not usually unduly crowded or thick with slums as was to happen later on. Town houses still stood pleasantly among gardens, orchards and farmyards. The towns still played a part in agricultural life, as well as being centres of trade and industry. Outside the protection of the town walls, which distinguished towns from open villages, there was usually an unfenced town-field where citizens who were part-time farmers grew corn on their strips of land and common pasture on which they grazed their cattle and sheep. At harvest-time journeymen and apprentices could be called on to lay down their crafts and help to gather in the corn. Even London was no exception to this part-country life.

However, these little half-rural towns had developed systems of self-government and independence that made life in them completely different from life in the villages. Trade made them prosperous and, with their money, they were willing to pay to free themselves from the restrictions and obligations imposed by lords of the manor. To obtain the privileges of self-government and control of local trade, the town had to be granted a Charter by the King or a Lord, Abbot or Bishop. Such a Charter could be awarded to a town in return for a large sum of money. Greatly prized privileges included freedom of the townsmen from all feudal dues and services, payment for land being by money rent only, and the right to own and dispose of property how they wished. The townsmen would usually be allowed to elect a council to organize local government, to regulate trade, probably to hold a weekly market and sometimes to hold an annual fair.

Because the hours of work were long, there was not much time for sports and entertainment, though Sunday was a day of rest and a number of Saints' days were holidays. Betting on the result of contests in shooting, wrestling, running and hurling stones or iron bars was very popular. Archery practice at the butts was encouraged rather than football or hockey, because this meant that the skill of England's longbowmen was not likely to decline. Stage-plays, often organized by the gilds on religious topics, and games, pageants and revels of various kinds provided a welcome break from the daily grind.

8 Practice at archery was encouraged.

The Life of a Yeoman Farmer in Birmingham

For most small farmers living in their villages, the order of life seemed to be fixed. It was difficult for a man to raise himself from being a villein or a serf to become a free yeoman and, even if that step was taken, it was still more difficult to become a prosperous landowner. However, the opportunities for trade inevitably led to change. In 1150 Peter Fitzwilliam acquired the manor of Bremengeham (Birmingham) in Warwickshire from Lord Dudley. In 1166, most unusually for a village, he was granted a Charter by Henry II, allowing him to hold a weekly market and collect market tolls. This opportunity to sell any surplus produce gave Bremengeham a head-start over other and larger villages around. In the thirteenth century a further Charter was obtained, permitting fairs to be held. These events attracted people from farther afield and caused the village to become a lively and prosperous community. Villeins and new inhabitants were encouraged to seek "rights of burgage" (tenancies of land), while the lord could easily find labourers to work for wages on his land and pay them from his rents. Freed from the burdens of compulsory land service, the villagers now had plenty of opportunity to develop crafts and trades. They could learn their skills as farmers or craftsmen from their fathers or neighbours and were not restricted by the rules of the town craft gilds.

During the fourteenth century the Lord of Birmingham and some prosperous villagers raised enough money to endow a stone-built priory. By now the village had formed close links with its coal- and iron-producing neighbours, which was to be very important in the future. It was a village of growing commercial activities and prosperous yeomen farmers.

Early in the fifteenth century the yeomen founded a religious organization called the Gild of the Holy Cross, with a Gild Hall for meetings, feasts and entertainments. The Gild looked after the old, the sick and the needy and built twelve almshouses for poor persons. Again unusually, the village was not run by a strong manorial lord but the people were left free to organize many of the local affairs communally and independently.

The Life of a Rich Merchant in London

In the medieval towns it was easier than in the country for a man to better himself and to change his position in society through hard work and enterprise. A villein was still not free to leave his village, but if he ran away and remained undiscovered for a year and a day he became a free man. Nevertheless, there were problems about making one's way in the town, where life was hedged round with rules and regulations. Most townsmen were craftsmen or merchants who belonged to gilds for their trades, into which outsiders could not easily enter. There were two types of gilds — craft gilds, set up by craftsmen like bakers, tailors or carpenters, and merchant gilds, formed by traders like grocers or fishmongers. Both types aimed to maintain standards of workmanship and fair trading and to protect their members; both limited the numbers allowed to join, and helped their members and their families in times of trouble. The craft gilds organized training schemes whereby their members had to serve an apprenticeship, become journeymen and pass tests before they could be accepted as master craftsmen.

A rich merchant like Richard Whittington (in real life rather different from the panto-

9   Portrait of Richard Whittington (1350-1427). ▶

12

Huius sparsa viri toti benefacta per ....sa monstrant indice qualis erat

The true portraicture of *RICHARD WHITINGTON* thrise Lord Maior
of London a vertuous and godly man full of good Works (and those famous) he builded
the Gate of London called Newegate, which before was a miserable doungeon. He builded
Whitington Colledge & made it an Almose house for poore people. Also he builded a
greate parte of y'e hospitall of S. Bartholomewes in westsmithfield in London. He also
builded the beautifull Library at y'e Gray Friers in Londō, called Christes Hospitall;
Also he builded the Guilde Halle Chappell and increased a greate parte of the East
ende of the saied halle, beside many other good workes.

R. Elstrack sculpsit

mime character), who was three times mayor of London, had a very different life-style from a yeoman farmer in Birmingham. He was the third son of a Gloucestershire Knight and came to London to make his fortune. As a member of the Mercer's Company, he supplied cloth of gold and other rich materials to the Court and made so much money that he was able to make enormous loans to Richard II, Henry IV and Henry V. He lived with his wife, Alice, in a fine mansion in the city which was quite as grand as the town houses lived in by nobles and bishops. He had no children to inherit his fortune and so he left money to endow two libraries, towards the rebuilding of Newgate prison, the repairing of Saint Bar-

10 Richard Whittington's almshouses, College Hill, London.
▼

tholomew's Hospital and of the Guildhall, and to build almshouses for thirteen poor people.

In the towns local government was much more independent than in the country. The mayor was the chief citizen, presiding over the elected council and sitting as a magistrate in the Court. The council appointed officials to maintain law and order and enforce local bye-laws, such as preventing strangers buying or selling goods unless they paid local tolls. The towns, especially London, were self-governing almost to the point of being independent states. A mayor like Richard Whittington, assisted by two sheriffs, directed the affairs of the City of London much as they ran their own gilds, though on a larger scale.

Sanitary arrangements and reliable clean water supplies were perhaps not too inadequate in villages like Birmingham, but the same standards were rather more alarming when applied to the larger numbers in towns. Houses were huddled close together within the protecting walls of the medieval town, and animals and poultry often wandered through the narrow, winding and very dirty streets. Rubbish and buckets of dirty water were thrown out of the houses into the streets and there was rarely any regular cleaning of the streets or removal of refuse. In London, however, most houses had proper drainage; there were public baths maintained by the city, and from about 1350 water was brought into the city in pipes from wells and streams outside the walls. Richard Whittington was one of several wealthy benefactors who provided conduits (channels or pipes) for pure water. Although these public services in London were quite advanced for the time, they were not enough to keep the city healthy. There were frequent outbreaks of the plague which culminated in the Black Death of 1349. That year even the tiniest village was unsafe, though usually over the next three centuries, when towns and cities were attacked, the villages were relatively free of infection.

14

2
The Late Seventeenth and Early Eighteenth Centuries

A Golden Age?

By the end of the Tudor period the population of England and Wales had reached over 4 million, four-fifths living in the country and only one-fifth in towns. In the country, there were a number of craftsmen in the villages and men employed, for instance, in the woollen cloth trade or as miners or quarrymen, but the bulk of the population cultivated land or tended animals. The high price of wool led many landowners to enclose their land, in order to change over from arable farming to pasture for sheep. Many tenants were evicted from their land, by trickery or force, and common land was often just taken over by the lords of the manor. The amount of land actually enclosed for sheep farming was probably as low as 2 per cent of the total area of England and Wales, but it caused a great outcry and much hardship in many districts, leading to unemployment and depopulation of whole villages. However, for most of the country the pattern of life was much the same as in the middle of the fourteenth century. Even those who lived in the towns were still often part-time farmers. Town populations were growing; York, Norwich and Bristol were exceptionally big and flourishing, with perhaps 30,000 inhabitants in each by the end of the seventeenth century. London, above all, which was a great centre of trade for home and abroad, may have had as many as 200,000 inhabitants.

Towards the end of the seventeenth century and during the early years of the eighteenth century — the period before the Agricultural and Industrial Revolutions — has sometimes been looked back on as a Golden Age for country people. It has been seen as the last age of solid, stable, rural England, the last age before invention, the machine and the factory made England mainly industrial instead of mainly agricultural. It was perhaps a breathing space before the

11 Seventeenth-century Bristol.

15

▲
12 Liverpool in the seventeenth century.

Dancing a Jig

▲
13 A rather optimistic impression of country pleasures in the early eighteenth century.

vast and painful upheaval of the Industrial Revolution; a time which still had continuity with the past and some concern for members of communities that shared a common heritage. But the villagers whose lives tottered on the edge of serious poverty would probably have been surprised to know that their life-time would later be seen as a "golden age". Indeed, Gregory King, who in the 1680s made estimates of the population and the incomes of various classes, claimed that of the 5½ million who now composed England and Wales more than half had expenses higher than their incomes and they could only make up the difference from "poor relief, charity and plunder".

By contrast, in the late seventeenth century, trade in towns was flourishing and industry was growing. Birmingham and Sheffield, for instance, were making advances in the iron and steel industry, Liverpool had become an extremely prosperous port for the new cotton trade, and Coventry and Macclesfield were famous for their silk. Bristol and Norwich now had over 30,000 inhabitants each; Yarmouth and Harwich had large ship-building yards; and Hull was growing, with its whaling and fishing industries. London was still dominant, but other towns were beginning to catch up.

Bledington, Gloucestershire

The development of the village of Bledington in Gloucestershire has been researched in detail by a recent historian.* She reports that the village, which at the time of Domesday Book had about 90 inhabitants, had a population of 179 just before the Black Death and some 270 persons in the late seventeenth century. By the late seventeenth century, apart from the big landlords, there were a number of yeomen farmers, some craftsmen, a few independent labourers and a large number of poor labourers. The power of the landlords had been growing. The break-up of the large estates and the enclosure of some of the open fields for sheep pasture made the old feudal courts out of date and their work was taken over by magistrates' courts. Minor cases were heard by Justices of the Peace, often in their own homes, while more important ones came before the Justices of the County, at the Quarter Sessions in a nearby country town. Whereas in the feudal courts juries of neighbours had heard evidence and helped in judgement, now magistrates, who were all landlords and later also prosperous clergymen, acted alone.

None of the yeomen farmers of Bledington held more than about 120 acres of land, but because of the increasing population in the towns and the demand for surplus food, they were modestly prosperous. Farming was still a communal activity in the open fields, and the crops had changed very little since medieval times. But a long series of good harvests and good prices for corn made the farmers better off than in

*M.K. Ashby, *The Changing English Village 1066-1914* (Roundwood Press, 1974)

▲
14   Banks Farm House on the village green at Bledington, the grounds of which contain the site of a Roman dwelling and of the old village meeting place (Town Banks) and the butts, where archery was practised. By the early seventeenth century the family living there was one of the three most prosperous in the village.

the past. Many of the farmhouses had been or were being rebuilt with fine windows and doorways and more rooms. The Mince family, for example, had three bedrooms, a kitchen and parlour, two butteries, a dairy and a cheeseroom. In 1691 John Mince was the first yeoman in Bledington to have a wagon and, when he died, he had a number of items of silver to leave in his will. Inside the house, too, there was more furniture and equipment. One notable change at this period was that stone slabs were taking the place of mud floors in the farmhouses, and the rushes were being swept out of doors.

In the Middle Ages the people of Bledington had a number of sports and competitions of skill which took place on the village green. And they were famous for their Morris dancers. During the Civil War and the Puritan period these village games and dances declined, though later they were revived. Bledington still has its Maypole on the green round which country dances are performed and still has a notable team of Morris Men and their own dance, Bledington Hey Away.

Samuel Pepys' London

In great contrast to the quiet but reasonably comfortable life of a yeoman farmer in Gloucestershire, we will consider the way of life described by the diarist, Samuel Pepys, who lived in London between 1633 and 1703. He came from a humble tailor's family, but had some wealthy relations, one of whom was able to get him a good position as a civil servant in the Navy Board. His own career is not remarkable, but the diary he kept (in code, to prevent others reading it) for nine years from 1660 to 1669 is an invaluable account of the events and fashions of London at an exceptionally interesting time.

Pepys' London had half a million inhabitants, mostly crowded inside the medieval walls with densely packed houses, shops and warehouses, narrow streets and a hundred churches. Outside the city walls were the growing suburbs and the Palace of Westminster, the residence of the King and his Court. Most houses had timber frames filled in with lath and plaster. They had little in the way of sanitation, and household water came from wells or conduits supplied by the Thames or other dubious sources. The houses were very close together, and the upper storeys overhung the ones below, so that the narrow streets were dim and airless and very smelly as refuse was still just thrown into the street.

The streets of London were packed with jostling crowds of merchants, workmen, servants, porters and street-traders, as well as private coaches for the rich, hackney coaches for hire, and carts and wagons for transporting goods. Pepys was very proud when in November 1668 he was able to order a "little chariott. . . covered with leather" that would hold four people. There was already a problem of traffic jams. Much use, however, was made of the river, for carrying both passengers and loads.

15 Portrait of Samuel Pepys, 1697.
▼

16 One of the new London Coffee Houses.
▼

17 Flight of townspeople into the country to escape from the Plague.

London had hundreds of taverns, ale-houses and inns, open all hours of the day and night. Pepys called in at one or two of them on most days for a drink of ale or wine or for a meal and to hear the current news and gossip. Tea, coffee and chocolate were newly fashionable drinks at this time. Pepys tasted tea for the first time in 1660 and he frequented the new coffee houses which were springing up in London.

Pepys worked very hard at his job, but also enjoyed entertaining and being entertained to meals by his friends. He loved going to the theatre, once seeing thirty plays in three months. Londoners were very happy when the theatres, which had been closed during Cromwell's time, re-opened at the Restoration of Charles II. Blood-thirsty sports like bear-baiting and cock-fighting were also brought back and there were puppet-plays and big annual fairs with side-shows, jugglers and other entertainments. But in Pepys' time many people made their own entertainment and he wrote in his diary: "Music is the thing of all the world that I love best." He and his friends often sang and played their instruments together. Pepys himself played the viol, lute, flageolet and recorder as well as taking lessons in singing and musical composition. He and his wife attended church on Sundays; he enjoyed the organ music, but sometimes went to sleep if the sermons were too long.

In the hot summer of 1665 the Plague swept through London killing 70,000 people. Pepys sent his wife to stay in Woolwich, but he remained for most of the time in the city and recorded the unhappy story. Early in 1666 people began to appear in the streets again and the shops to re-open. Later in the year a new disaster struck — the Great Fire of London. Over 13,000 houses, 70 churches, St Paul's Cathedral, the Guildhall and Exchange and countless shops and warehouses were destroyed. Plans were made to rebuild a modern city with wider streets, but in the end little came of them and the new London mostly followed the pattern of the old.

18 Reconstruction of the Great Fire of London, 1666.

3
The Agricultural
and Industrial Revolutions

A Revolution in Farming

During the eighteenth century the population of England and Wales grew steadily and, by the first official Census in 1801, it had reached nearly nine million. With more mouths to feed, good profits could be made out of farming. Home food supplies could be increased in two ways; firstly, by cutting down woodland, reclaiming wasteland and draining the Fen lands; secondly, by introducing more efficient methods of farming — new crops and crop rotations, new machines, better drainage and enrichment of the soil and scientific stock breeding. A number of "improving landlords" popularized such ideas as Lord Townshend's Norfolk Four Course Crop Rotation, which included turnips and clover and cut out the waste of the fallow field, and Jethro Tull's seed drill and horse hoe, which enabled fields to be weeded and increased productivity. Robert Bakewell, Coke of Holkham and the Colling brothers gave a lead on selective stock breeding which resulted in great improvements in the quality of livestock. But all these changes could not be made while the open fields remained, and in the early years of the century three-fifths of the cultivated land was still farmed in this way.

Widespread enclosure of the land became necessary. This meant landowners securing their land in one piece, with fences or hedges round it, instead of having it scattered in the open fields. Enclosure by private strip-swapping arrangements and by buying land for sheep pasture had been going on slowly for centuries, but after 1750 it speeded up. Except when all the parties agreed to make a private enclosure arrangement, permission to enclose an open-field village had to be obtained by an individual Act of Parliament. The procedure favoured the big landowners, who might be "gentlemen farmers" enthusiastic to introduce new methods or absentee landlords, but who both hoped to make large profits and to enjoy the social importance and political power that went with landownership. These landowners often added to their holdings by taking over commons, woodland and waste and buying up the land of small tenants who might be unaware of what was happening until too late. When the Parliamentary Commissioners arrived to supervise the dividing-up of the spoils, the villagers often could not afford to pay the legal and other expenses and, in any case, without their share of the common land, could not make a living. Many small freeholders and tenant farmers were forced to sell their land for very unfair prices, and they either became landless

19 Country people leaving their village in the days ▶ of enclosure.

labourers or moved to the towns to find work in the new factories. The labourers, too, lost their customary rights to use the waste and woodland and to glean after the harvest. A large number of villagers became completely destitute and dependent on the Poor Law.

The Agricultural Revolution certainly achieved a great increase in food production, which enabled Britain to feed its growing population and prevented the country being starved into surrender during the war with France (1793-1815). But this success was gained at the cost of great distress and hardship for a large number of villagers.

Even Arthur Young, who was a great supporter of modern improvements and enclosure, was bound to admit that "by nineteen out of twenty enclosure acts, the poor are injured, sometimes grossly injured". He overheard a villager in an ale-house say: "If I am sober, shall I have land for a cow? If I am frugal, shall I have an acre of potatoes?. . . You offer me . . . nothing but a parish officer and a workhouse. Bring me another pot!" And another bewildered man remarked: "All I know is I had a cow and an Act of Parliament took it from me."

Although landowners were doing well and rents were soaring, the wages of farm labourers were falling and their condition was pitiful. The families no longer had any land on which to grow vegetables or where they could keep animals or poultry. They no longer had the right to collect fuel on the wasteland, and so their houses were cold

20 The eighteenth-century squire kept all the sport of hunting and shooting animals and birds for himself and his friends, and enforced savage punishment for poachers.
▼

21 A poacher caught in a "humane" man trap.
▼

and hot meals were infrequent. They could not afford to buy much food at the shops where prices were high. Their main diet was bread and tea. There was no money to spare for clothes. Numbers died from weakness caused by being cold and from outright starvation.

The big landowners now claimed the exclusive right to the sport of shooting birds and animals on the land, and the Game Laws imposed harsh penalties on "poachers". The half-starved labourers who tried to catch a hare or rabbit for their hungry families might be sentenced to whipping, imprisonment, transportation or even death. And when it was clear that even these penalties would not deter the countryman from poaching, the landlords planted man-traps and spring-guns to break their spirits. The poacher who was caught was brought before a magistrate, who was unlikely to show any mercy, as he was inevitably one of the local landowners who delighted in hunting and shooting.

During the war with France, conditions for the villagers grew worse. A shortage of corn made the price of bread rise sharply, but wages did not keep pace with prices. The upper classes even had some fear of revolution like the one in France. In 1795 a group of magistrates met at Speenhamland in Berkshire to work out the minimum wage on which a country labourer could exist in their district. They drew up a scale based on the price of bread and the number in the family. The plan was that, if a man was working and his wages were below the allowance worked out for his family, the parish would make up the amount; if he was totally unemployed, the parish would pay out the whole allowance. If the price of bread went up or down, the allowance would be adjusted.

It was never intended that the Speenhamland system should be nationally adopted, but it was, in fact, widely copied. The effect of this well-intentioned idea was disastrous — you got the same money whether you

22 The domestic or cottage system: carding and spinning yarn in the home.

worked or not, wages were kept low, the poor rate rocketed and a large proportion of country people became dependent on charity.

The Industrial Revolution

In the early eighteenth century England was still a mainly rural country; manufacturing was local and on a small scale and was less important than farming. The sixteenth and seventeenth centuries had seen the rise of trading companies and the success of the great merchant adventurers. The founding of colonies and the growth of merchant shipping opened up new opportunities to make money from overseas trade. As time went on, the old methods of production were unable to take full advantage of these possibilities and there followed, therefore, a period of change and invention generally known as the "Industrial Revolution".

Before the eighteenth century most goods were made in the home or workshop, with their own tools, by people who were often part-time farmers. Wives and children spun the wool into thread and the men wove it into cloth. However, in some parts of the country since the sixteenth century the woollen cloth trade had been organized by merchants with money to put into businesses; these merchants distributed the raw materials, collected the completed bales of cloth and sold the finished product. Some merchants set up large workshops and provided the looms and other tools. The cotton industry in Lancashire and the silk industry in London, Derby and Macclesfield also set up small factories of this kind. Quite early in the eighteenth century water power began to be used in some of the textile mills.

But first there had to be some major improvements in the methods of transport. By the end of the eighteenth century hundreds of new turnpike roads, well surfaced and drained, linked the main centres of trade and fashion. These were excellent for transporting people and the mail, but not too good for heavy, bulky or fragile loads. A little later a network of canals was made to provide a system of transport for the raw materials, machinery and the manufactured goods, which was necessary for the vast expansion of industry and trade.

As in the case of the Agricultural Revolution, the main reason for change was the opportunity to make money. Merchants could sell more goods abroad and to the growing population at home; they were prepared to use the profits they had made from trade, to improve the methods of production. This led to the invention of a

▲
24 Rawsfolds Mill. This was the first Yorkshire Mill to have modern machinery introduced about 1811 and here rioting by the Luddites and attacks on the machinery took place.

▲
25 Tyburn Turnpike, 1820, near to Marble Arch, London.

26 Stour Port, on the Staffordshire and Worcestershire Canal.
▼

23 The domestic system: weaving cloth. Apprentices working looms.
▼

large number of machines and processes which caused factories to replace cottage industry and led to independent craftsmen becoming wage-earners and to the movement of people from the country to the factory towns. By 1790 one-third of the population had become town dwellers.

The industrial towns were bleak, unhealthy and smoky. Builders out for quick profits put up houses which soon became slums. Arrangements for sewage disposal, water supply or burials, which might have seemed adequate in the villages, became a serious danger in the overcrowded towns. Many men could not find work in the towns and families were often kept from starvation by the labour of the women and children who worked very long hours in appalling conditions.

Britain's industrial towns grew up around the mines, mills and factories which sprang up on the coalfields, where there were other mineral deposits and at ports where raw materials were imported and finished goods exported. The cotton industry in Lancashire, the woollen industry in Yorkshire, iron and steel in Sheffield, pottery around Stoke-on-Trent and metal working in Birmingham were some of the centres of this Industrial Revolution. Villages were transformed almost overnight, it seemed, into sprawling towns. Oldham, for instance, grew from a village of 300 inhabitants to a town of 17,000 between 1750 and 1800; Manchester had under 10,000 people in 1700 but by 1800 it had 95,000 inhabitants.

27 "Jack in the Green" procession and celebrations in Upper Lisson Street, Paddington, London, in the early nineteenth century. Country customs were still followed in the towns.

"The Princely" Matthew Boulton of Birmingham

In the Middle Ages Birmingham was a prosperous village which was already outstripping many villages around, as a result of its markets and fairs and because of the nearby deposits of iron and coal which encouraged ironsmiths to set up forges. (See page 12.) By the seventeenth century a number of smithies made every sort of iron, brass and copper ware. During the second half of the seventeenth century Birmingham trebled in size from 5,000 to 15,000 inhabitants. Much-needed improvements were made in road and river transport and later, Birmingham was said to have more canals than Venice.

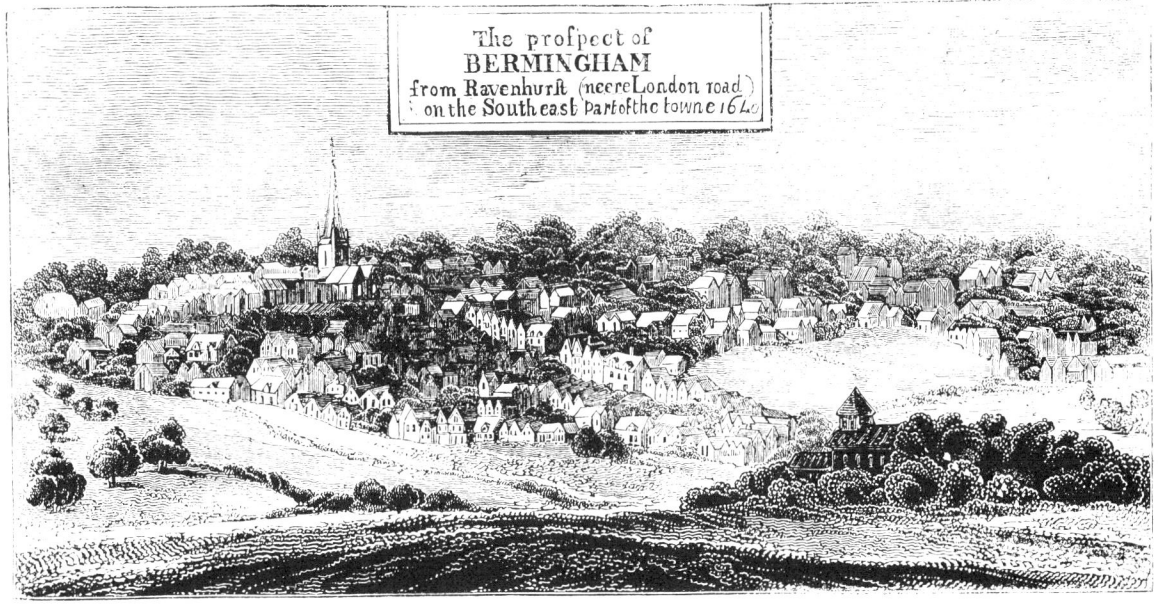

The prospect of
BERMINGHAM
from Ravenhurst (neere London road)
on the South east part of the towne 1640

28 Birmingham in 1640.

29 A similar view of Birmingham in 1795.

Matthew Boulton was born in Birmingham in 1728, the son of a manufacturer of buttons and buckles, items for which the town was already world-famous, along with "toys" (this term meant any useful lightweight manufactured article), jewellery and guns. He was thirty-one when he took over his father's factory, and soon ran into financial problems as a result of his over-ambitious manufacturing plans. His marriage to Anne Robinson, the daughter of a wealthy Lichfield family, brought him a dowry of £28,000 and when after three years she died, Boulton married Anne's sister and his financial standing was now secure. He employed an architect to design his famous Soho works, which became a national showpiece of advanced engineering skill when it opened in 1762. In 1775 he went into partnership with James Watt, the inventor of the steam engine, Watt providing the inventive genius and "the princely Boulton", as Watt described him, the business skill. As one writer has put it, this linked "the captain of industry with the scientist-inventor".

At the Soho works revolutionary methods of specialization of labour and training of the workpeople to produce accurate machine parts led to an increase in output to ten times greater than the average at that time. The factory turned out taps, machine parts, candlesticks, lamps, silverware, buttons, ornaments and clocks and dozens of useful and decorative items.

James Watt was able to improve his steam engine using the up-to-date resources of the Soho works. In 1776 his first satisfactory engine was completed, and in 1781 he

30 Matthew Boulton's Soho Works, Birmingham.
▼

31 The Lamplighter, 1808. ➤

Published by William Miller, Albemale Street, Jan't 1805.

patented the method of using the engine to turn a wheel and so drive machinery. The Boulton-Watt partnership which produced steam power to drive innumerable new machines was one of the most important contributions to the Industrial Revolution. No wonder that Boulton is reported to have said proudly to the visiting George III, who asked what happened at the Soho works, "I sell, Sire, what all the world desires, power." Boulton died in 1809, aged eighty-one. For men like these, Birmingham was a place of great opportunity. It was not, however, until 1838 that a Charter of Incorporation made the town a parliamentary borough and allowed it to elect a town council. Between 1769 and 1847 (when the town obtained effective power to run its own affairs) the town was administered by fifty Street Commissioners who ran a central market and controlled street lighting and public works; they even built public baths, a mental hospital and a prison.

Boulton and Watt had a number of friends of power and influence among Birmingham's growing number of successful manufacturers, bankers, inventors and businessmen. Naturally, many of these men met socially and shared their professional experience with one another. In 1776, for example, the Lunar Society (meeting monthly at the full moon, which made it easier to travel home at night) was set up to exchange news on scientific matters, but also on literature and art. Matthew Boulton, James Watt, Dr Erasmus Darwin, Dr Joseph Priestley, and Josiah Wedgwood were among the distinguished founder members. One of the causes to which the Society gave vigorous support was the cutting of canals which they saw as invaluable for better communications and increased trade with other parts of the country.

32 A meeting of the Lunar Society.
▼

A writer in 1783 described his first view of Boulton's Birmingham as "uncrowded with houses, untarnished with smoke"; he admired the "modern architecture" and said the buildings on the outskirts of the town "rose in a style of elegance". He found it a large and vigorous place, with a "happy people", and "full of industry", meaning industriousness or great activity. But the townspeople played hard as well as working hard. There was prize-fighting, cock-fighting, fives, quoits, skittles and ale for the factory workers; for the general public there was horse-racing in the streets and bull-baiting in the Bull Ring; for the gentry there were bowls and entertainment in each other's homes, concerts and expeditions to beauty spots in the country.

A Farmer in Bledington, Gloucestershire*

The open-field village of Bledington was enclosed in 1769. Before this time there had been some strip-swapping to get some of the farmers' land into more compact pieces in the open fields. Richard Baker's holding of 250 strips in 1711, for instance, consisted of thirty groups of three or two strips and 184 strips scattered singly. The villagers seemed to be in no hurry to change. Bledington was on the whole slow to adopt new farming methods such as planting artificial grasses and turnips and experimenting with selective stock breeding. However, the farmers were more prosperous than before and were investing some of their money in building barns and improving their farmsteads.

* See page 17 for Bledington in the seventeenth century.

33 Hogarth's impression of cock-fighting.

In the houses there was more furniture and equipment, providing a higher degree of comfort, elegance and cleanliness.

Late in 1768 a petition was presented to Parliament by the Dean and Chapter of Christ Church, Oxford, the Chancellor, Masters and Students of Oxford University, Mr Ambrose Reddall, five other named commoners "and others" (thirteen in all) to allow a Bill for the enclosure of Bledington to be presented. Owners of at least two-thirds of the land at Bledington had to sign the petition for it to go forward and, though there was some opposition, it was on a small scale. The petition was accepted without question and five Members of Parliament were "ordered" to prepare a Bill. This was quickly and efficiently done. The customary rights of the poor to use common land could not be legally proved and so they were abolished. Two charitable arrangements were made: first, six acres of furze land were set aside for the poor to use for collecting fuel; and secondly, a small plot of land was granted to the vicar. Another 140 acres were quite unusually left unenclosed and to be divided into strips, proportionately to the "commoners'" previous holdings — it was a sort of open field in miniature which meant, at least, that all small farmers still had some land.

The Parliamentary Commissioners first worked out where the roads and paths should be made and then awarded each commoner compensation for his rights in the open fields, bearing in mind not only the acreage but also the fertility and conven-ience for working. Exchanges of land awarded were allowed, to give the farmers their land as much in one piece as possible. For instance, Mary Coombs, a widow, made three exchanges to get her 19 acres stretching from her own back door and extending to the outskirts of the village in three, long, narrow, but connected fields.

The poorer farmers had two anxieties; how to pay for the cost of the Award and how to pay or provide for the fencing of their fields. The cost of the Award, including the lawyer from Gloucester, the surveyor and assistants, and the Commissioners, was nearly £1,000, which worked out at about 16s. 6d. an acre, though it varied according to the valuation of the particular land. Mary Coombs got her 19 acres for £21 and Mr Reddall paid £278 for his 393 acres. The fencing was mostly done with hurdles, to be followed by planted hawthorn hedges.

Most of the commoners who received a few acres managed to survive in Bledington during the next few years, though among the labourers there was an increase in poverty and misery. The old system had been rooted in communal farming and co-operation; now it was every family for itself. In 1807, thirty-eight years after enclosure, there were 19 holdings in the village. Mrs Coombs had sold her cleverly planned little farm to another woman who put in tenants; a year later it was absorbed into Oxford University's farm.

34 An eighteenth-century travelling fair provided simple amusements for villagers.
▼

4
Late Victorian
Town and Country Life

Town and Country Houses

Between 1801 and 1851 the population of England and Wales doubled, to reach 18 million, more than half of whom lived in the towns; by 1881 the population had grown to 26 million, two-thirds of whom were town-dwellers. As there had been no local authority control over building, houses, factories and warehouses were put up hugger-mugger together without restriction. The factories belched forth smoke and dirt over the densely packed jerry-built workers' houses. Speculative builders might cram as many as 125 houses on to a single acre. The houses were very small, often only three rooms for families with as many as 10 or 12 children. Some families all lived in one room and some in dark, damp cellars. Some of the houses were "back-to-back" with no back doors or yards; some were in long terraces and some round courtyards; there were no dustmen and often no drains and probably one water tap for a row of houses.

Living conditions for agricultural workers and their families were just as overcrowded and lacking in amenities as they were for town workers but at least there was fresh air and the countryside around their picturesque, if insanitary cottages. However,

despite the appalling housing conditions in the Victorian towns, the poorer classes were better off in some respects than they had been before and infinitely better off than those who remained in the country and worked on the farms; their wages were higher and they could afford more meat, bread and fruit. Women and children in the country had to help out weeding, stone-picking, bird-scaring and at harvest-time, though they were only paid a pittance. Once a farm labourer's daughter reached about the age of twelve, her family would be likely to try to find her "a place" as a domestic servant.

The homes of businessmen, factory owners and professional people, such as doctors and lawyers, were of quite a different standard from those of working people. They were usually large, built on the outskirts of the town and with good gardens. Many followed the new mock Gothic style of architecture, with turrets and gables and stained glass windows. These houses had several bedrooms, a bathroom and flushing lavatory and quarters for servants. In 1851 there were over a million domestic servants in England and Wales, nearly two-thirds of them coming from country homes. An upper-class home might have eight or ten servants ranging from butler and housekeeper down to scullery maid and "boots".

31

Public Health

It soon became clear that the working-class houses flung up without forethought in the early years of the Industrial Revolution had provided the Victorians with a legacy of slums and dangerous disease. The problems of sanitation and sewage would not solve themselves and even the middle classes in their clean and comfortable homes were not immune from the epidemics of cholera, typhus and smallpox which were causing a steep increase in the death rate in towns. Nevertheless, it was most dangerous of all to live in the poorer central districts of the

35   The backyards of London, 1878.
▼

towns: in 1840 in Manchester, for instance, the death rate in the middle-class suburb of Broughton was 15.8 per 1,000; nearer to the town centre it was 28.6, and in the centre it was 35.2. The average age of death of workers in Manchester was seventeen years. But, to begin with, it was not understood that the overcrowded, insanitary conditions were responsible for disease.

In 1835 the Municipal Corporations Act reformed some aspects of local government in the towns. It introduced democratically elected borough councils, though their powers were mostly limited to providing a police force and street paving and lighting. Any health or sanitary improvements

36 The vicarage at Burgess Hill, London, c.1870.

▲
37 Extreme poverty in Ireland in the 1840s led
many thousands of starving and sick people to
flock to England and make conditions in the slums
even worse.

38 Leeds in the late nineteenth century had ►
imposing civic buildings and fine shops.

required a special Act of Parliament. Outbreaks of cholera in 1832 and 1837 caused
serious alarm and so the government set
up a Royal Commission on the Health of
Towns which reported in 1844 and 1845.

After the potato famine in Ireland in
1846 hundreds of thousands of Irish landed
in England, many starving and destitute and
already suffering from infectious diseases.
In 1851 about 17 per cent of the population of Liverpool was Irish, who in their
distress were driven to accept even lower
pay and more squalid living conditions
than the English poor would do. As many as
sixty people were found in one house con-
taining four small rooms, and in another case
more than forty people were found sleeping
in a cellar.

A Central Board of Health was set up in
1848 but not given enough power to be

effective. Some of the worst conditions,
however, were remedied by separate Acts
of Parliament in the 1850s and '60s, which
dealt with removal of refuse, provision of
sewers, smoke nuisance, workmen's lodgings
and measures to prevent epidemics and contagious diseases. Further Acts in the 1870s
allowed local authorities to knock down
slums and rehouse their inhabitants and
compelled them to appoint Medical Officers
of Health, to provide hospitals and to organize local sanitary services.

The Effect of the Railways

Just as improvements in the roads and the
building of canals had made vast changes
in industrial and social life in the eighteenth
century, so after the 1840s and '50s the
railways revolutionized transport and had
many far-reaching effects on the develop-

39 A railway viaduct over the Preston Road in Brighton.

ment of towns. One very noticeable change was the spread of suburbs. Towns spread outwards as many people chose to live away from the town centres, in a cleaner and healthier atmosphere, and to travel to work by train. The poor, however, stayed in the old insanitary city centres. Where railway lines converged at large junctions, and where shunting yards and repair shops were built, whole new towns sprang up. Some country market towns like Swindon and Peterborough were transformed into cities by their railway workshops, while Crewe grew from a village of 203 people in 1841 to a town of more than 18,000 by 1871. Holiday towns grew up along the coast as a result of cheap and easy communication with densely populated areas. The cheap day excursion meant that even working-class families could have an occa-

sional day's outing to Southend, Blackpool or Scarborough and some managed to save up for a week's holiday. Hotels and boarding houses sprang up, piers and promenades were built, and amusements like donkey-rides, concert parties and slot machines were provided. Middle-class families could enjoy longer holidays on the more select beaches at resorts like Bournemouth, Southport and Bridlington.

The railways speeded everything up, leading to cheaper transport and wider markets. In the towns there was a great increase in retail shops which began to take the place of fairs. Men who were out of work could travel more easily to centres of employment and could send for their families to follow them when they found work. The railways did a great deal to unify the country, by carrying people and news and information. The punctual delivery of the daily paper, for instance, made people more aware of national, political and other issues. More people could read and write by now and the abolition of the tax on paper in 1855 brought down the price of newspapers, the first penny newspaper being published that year.

The railways also changed the "face and pace" of the countryside. Cuttings, embankments, bridges and viaducts, railway lines, signal boxes and stations transformed the rural landscape. Perishable goods like milk, market gardening produce and fruit could be carried quickly for long distances and fish ports like Grimsby grew when they could send their catch speedily to London and the industrial centres. Bulk deliveries of fertilizers and cattle food and new machinery such as reaping and threshing machines, steam ploughs, drills and mowers could now be easily transported. As for the agricultural

40 Scarborough.
▼

labourers, they lost some of their sense of isolation and in the 1870s many of them joined Joseph Arch's National Agricultural Labourers Union and made a brief but doomed attempt to unite to secure better wages for farm workers.

Transport within the towns was greatly improved. The upper classes still had their own private carriages, but there were also horse-drawn hansom cabs (introduced in the 1830s) or broughams (from the 1840s) which could be hired, and for working people there were horse-drawn omnibuses (from about 1830) and later also trams with quite low fares. By the end of the century an electrified underground railway system had been constructed in London, and trams in the big cities were driven by electricity.

Leisure and Pleasure

The opportunity to enjoy leisure activities very much depended on one's prosperity and social position. For those who could afford it, there were sports to take part in like croquet, tennis, archery and cycling and sporting activities to watch like cricket, football and horse-racing. In the towns there were theatres, music halls and restaurants. But many working-class families worked long hours for low wages and had neither the time nor the money for enter-

41 Agricultural strike meeting in Northampton-shire, 1872.

tainments. Because of their wretched lives, many working people spent money they could ill afford in public houses. A temperance campaign did achieve some improvement by pressing the government to strengthen the licensing laws and limit the opening hours of public houses.

In the country many of the old customs and festivals were still observed — May and harvest festivals, sheep-shearing suppers, agricultural shows and annual fairs. Many village activities were organized by the local church or chapel, though Sunday attendance was much less than in earlier days.

A church Census in 1851 revealed the "shocking" fact that, out of a population of 18 million, only seven and a quarter million attended some service on the day of the count. Great anxiety was expressed about the "heathendom" of the "dark masses of our uninstructed people", especially in the northern industrial towns. Great efforts were made to encourage the working classes to return to church by both Anglican and Non-conformist groups with a more modern approach to religious worship. Their campaigns met with only a limited response, but the lively Salvation Army founded by William Booth and his wife in 1865 as a "Christian Mission to the Heathen of our Own Country" was more successful.

However, some of the "uninstructed people" were applying their minds in other directions by joining Mechanics' Institutes where they could try to make up for their lack of early education and then go on to study a wide range of subjects. Public libraries could be provided by local authorities after 1845 and though they tended at first to close before working men had left their employment, opportunities for self-education were growing.

42 Electric tramway at Northfleet, London, 1889.
▼

43   Open-air ox-roast, Osney, Oxfordshire, for Queen Victoria's Golden Jubilee, 1887.

44   Selling Bibles at St Giles's Fair, Oxford, in about 1880.

Victorian Prosperity followed by the "Great Depression"

Up to the 1870s Britain's industry and trade were flourishing — Britain had had a head start over other countries in its "Industrial Revolution" and had profited from expanding production, cheaper transport and wider markets. However, some other nations who were Britain's rivals began to protect their own industries against the import of British goods and started producing similar goods as cheaply. By 1873 a period, called by some the "Great Depression", had set in. Prices and profits fell. Unemployment increased, but workers who had jobs were better off than before.

In the country the depression was worse than in the towns. As railways opened up the great plains of the USA, Canada, Australia, Russia and the Argentine and steamships speeded up sea-transport, cheap wheat and frozen meat (in refrigerated ships) began to flood the home market. Food prices fell, rents fell and so did the wages of farm workers. Large numbers of people left the country to find work in the towns and some emigrated to the colonies or America. Between 1871 and 1901 the number of agricultural workers fell by 30 per cent.

> **CONTRAST**: an Oxfordshire Village in the 1870s and 1880s and Poverty in the City of York at the Turn of the Century

"Lark Rise"

Flora Thompson's three books (put together as *Lark Rise to Candleford*) about her hamlet, nearest village and country town in the 1870s and 1880s describe vividly the last days of the old village life before it was swamped by the modern world. The village was only nineteen miles from Oxford, but that city was as remote to most villagers as New York might seem today. Laura, the chief character of the books, is Flora Thompson herself, who remembered hearing "Old Sally" talk about the days before the common land was enclosed.

The men of Lark Rise were farm labourers who had no land, apart from their gardens, but were wage-earners working long hours struggling to keep their families on very low incomes. The women went gleaning in the fields after the harvest, and with the grain they often baked their own wholemeal bread. Villagers were "largely self-supporting".

Every household grew its own vegetables, produced its new-laid eggs and cured its own bacon. Jams, jellies, wines and pickles were made at home as a matter of course.

Many households kept bees and "even the poor enjoyed a rough plenty".

Although their monotonous diet kept them fairly healthy, there was little money to spare for many necessities, like footwear and clothes, and none for amusements. May Day and Harvest Home were celebrated in the village, with feasts and games and the most memorable occasion of all was Queen Victoria's Golden Jubilee in 1887.

Most of the cottages at Lark Rise were small stone-built boxes with tiled roofs, though a few were thatched. They had one room downstairs and one or two bedrooms, often divided by a curtain, to separate the children from their parents. It was a very tight fit when there were eight or ten children. Big boys might sleep downstairs or with a neighbour; big girls were nearly always sent away to work in service. The cottages were not slums, however, because the women scrubbed endlessly and kept the doors and windows open whenever the weather permitted, and the family lived in the open air when possible. Most of the families kept a "cottage pig" in a shack in the garden. Pig killing was "a nasty bloody business", but

45 Women harvesters in Norfolk fields at the end of the nineteenth century.

46 Ploughmen with their teams of horses, 1880.

it provided the family with an important tasty food. There was no water supply to the cottages, but each house had a water butt to collect and store rain water from the roof; when this ran dry, the women had to

walk a distance to collect water from a well. The cottages' only sanitation were "privies" — pits with a seat over them — at the end of the gardens, and emptied only twice a year. Flora Thompson who said that "after the Jubilee nothing ever seemed quite the same" commented that then "the Sanitary Inspector appeared for the first time in the hamlet, and shook his head over the pigsties and privies".

The men and boys in the hamlet and village all worked for the same landlord who had combined several old farms. The men worked hard and steadily for "ten bob a week", ploughing, hedging, ditching, sheep-shearing, thatching or mowing, according to the season. Specialists like shepherds, stockmen and blacksmiths got an extra two shillings a week and a rent-free cottage near the farmstead; boys naturally earned less. Ploughs, drills and harrows were horse-drawn, but machinery was just coming into use with hired reapers and threshing machines. On Friday evenings the labourers, politely pulling their forelocks, were paid their wages by the farmer himself; he was considered "not a bad ole sort" who, unlike many, made no effort to influence the way they voted at elections, nor put pressure on them to go to church.

Once a man was too old to work, he and his wife often lived in daily fear of the workhouse. The Poor Law authorities allowed old people a small weekly sum as outdoor relief, but it was not enough to live on unless they had children to help them. Flora Thompson commented:

When, twenty years later, the Old Age Pensions began, life was transformed for such aged cottagers. They were relieved of anxiety. They were suddenly rich. Independent for life! . . . tears of gratitude would run down the cheeks of some . . . as they picked up their money at the Post Office. They said "God Bless that Lord George." (They could not believe anyone so powerful and generous could be plain Mr. Lloyd George) and "God bless you, miss" to the girl who handed them their money and to whom they gave flowers and apples from their gardens.

York at the End of the Nineteenth Century

The ancient and beautiful city of York with its medieval walls and famous Minster came under the spotlight of a detailed social study at the end of the nineteenth century. R. Seebohm Rowntree, who had been impressed by the exposures of Charles Booth's *The Life and Labour of the People of London* and other writers' work on the problem of poverty in London, planned to "throw some light upon the conditions which govern the life of the wage-earning classes" in York. It was an ambitious project involving house-to-house visits in 388 streets, to 11,560 families.

The main employment in York was in the railway workshops, the cocoa and confectionery works and lesser industries like flour milling and brewing. There was little unemployment, no difficulty for young people in finding work, but few highly paid jobs. Having gathered detailed information about the earnings and expenses of almost every wage-earning family, Rowntree calculated the minimum weekly income needed by families of various sizes for (i) food, (ii) rent, and (iii) all else. His figure for a "moderate family" of two adults and three children was 21s.8d. — 12s.9d. for food, 4s.0d. for rent, and 4s.11d. for clothing, light, fuel, etc. These calculations assumed the careful choice of the most nutritious food at the lowest current prices and were considered to be the absolute minimum to achieve "merely physical efficiency".

Rowntree found that 43.4 per cent of the wage-earners or 27.8 per cent of the

47 A view of York Minster from the north-east. Beneath the beauty of the city Rowntree discovered much poverty.

city's population fell below this "poverty line". He divided the families living in poverty into two groups: (a) "Primary Poverty", where families' total earnings were not enough to enable them to buy sufficient food and other minimum needs for health and efficiency. The numbers experiencing this standard of living, "stringent to severity though it is," said Rowntree, "& bare of all creature comforts", amounted to almost exactly 10 per cent of the total population of York. And (b) "Secondary Poverty", where total earnings would have been enough to keep the family healthy if some of the money had not been spent on something other than basic household needs, "either useful or wasteful". This group amounted to nearly 18 per cent of the population.

Some of the wasteful expenditure was money spent in York's 338 public houses — one for every 230 persons, but with, said Rowntree, an excessive number of them in the old, working-class districts. To illustrate one of the characteristics of slum life, he described the pattern of behaviour in Hungate, comparing "the reckless expenditure of money as soon as obtained, with the aggravated want at other times; the rowdy Saturday night, with the Monday morning pilgrimage to the pawnshop". But he did recognize that the bleak and dreary homes of poor people compared badly with the social attractions of the public houses which were well-lit, warm and often "gaudily, if cheaply decorated" and where there was cheerful company and often singing.

The results of the poverty in York were shown in the early years of the twentieth century in the very low standard of health revealed by the medical examination of schoolchildren (introduced in 1907) and the failure of many men who wanted to enlist in the army to reach the minimum physical standard required. Rowntree thought this was not surprising, as he estimated that the working classes on average received 25 per cent less food than scientific experts had proved to be necessary to maintain physical efficiency. He did not imply that the people were chronically hungry, but claimed that the food they ate was not sufficiently nutritious. Housing standards, too, were often deplorable. Six per cent of people were living with more than two persons to a room, with insufficient air space and sleeping accommodation. Water supplies and sewerage were dangerously inadequate. In fact, Rowntree said: "York contains slums as degrading and filthy as any to be found in London."

In his survey Rowntree gave some brief facts about a number of unnamed poor families. Although their anonymous stories are very basic, it does enable anyone with an imagination to construct some sort of picture of the life of poor families in towns at the turn of the century:

Families in "Class A" (i.e. Income at the level of under 18s. a week for a "moderate family" of 2 adults and 3 children

Labourer, Foundry. Married. Four rooms. Four children. Steady; work regular. Man has bad eyesight and poor wage accord-ingly. Family live in the midst of smoke. Rent (3s.) cheap on account of smoke.

Widow. Two rooms, Eleven children; the eldest was fifteen when father died, four now working. Sober and very indus-trious, clean and fairly comfortable. Never in debt. Children fairly well clothed and fed. Rooms well kept and of a good size. Parish relief. Rent 2s.6d.

Messenger. Married. Seven children. Three rooms, Husband delicate. Very dirty house. Wife works when able. This house shares one closet with one other house and one water tap with three other houses. Rent 3s.6d.

"Class D" family (income over 30s. a week for a "moderate family"

Painter, aged 40. Married. Two rooms. Two children of school age and under. Son (19) warehouseman, Son (15) labourer, Daughter (18) confectionery works. Overcrowded. Six houses share one water tap and three houses share one closet. Rent 2s.6d.

48 An example of poverty – this queue is waiting to buy trimmings of meat at cheap prices in 1901.

5
Two Wars
and the Years Between
(1914-1945)

Edwardian Contrasts

The early years of the twentieth century saw the "Great Depression" give way to Edward-ian progress and prosperity. For the wealthy upper and middle classes it was a comfort-able and exciting time, with the opportunity to take part in a great variety of pleasurable activities: going to theatres and balls, eating

and drinking expensive food and wines at fashionable restaurants, spending conspicuously on clothes and household things, attending the races at Ascot and Goodwood, joining house parties in the country, hunting, shooting and fishing on private estates, staying at luxury hotels and travelling at home and abroad. The arrival of the motor

49 Edwardian prosperity: tea with strawberries on the river terrace of the Houses of Parliament, 1902.

50 Edwardian poverty: Atherstone slums, Warwick.

▲
51 Hop pickers near Alton, Hampshire, 1912.

car gave the leisured classes great mobility; and as domestic servants were cheap, the better off could be waited on hand and foot.

This prosperity was only to be enjoyed by the wealthy, however, while the poor, both in town and country, were ill-clad, lived in cold, squalid homes and often did not have enough to eat. The seriousness of the condition of the poor had been revealed when 60 per cent of volunteers for the Boer War were rejected as physically unfit. Some improvements were made — better public health facilities and medical care introduced. A school medical service was started in 1907, and from 1906 school meals could be provided for the needy, but the gulf between the "haves" and the "have-nots" had never seemed wider nor more resented. In 1908 old age pensions were introduced for people over seventy with very low incomes (5s. a week or 7s.6d. for a couple), and in 1911 a National Insurance Scheme made limited payments to contributors in sickness or un-

employment. To pay for these modest measures to help the poor, the government had to increase the taxes on the rich, many of whom protested. Lloyd George, the Prime Minister, said that his Budget, which set out these new proposals, was "a war budget. It is for raising money, " he declared, "to wage warfare on poverty and squalor."

The First World War and After

In August 1914 the major European powers embarked on a war which they all claimed was necessary for their own defence. Austria-Hungary and Germany were on one side and Russia, France and Great Britain on the other. Everyone had expected that great decisive battles would be fought, but after a German advance through Belgium into

52 Street scene in Wigan, Lancashire, where in ➤ 1939 10 out of 15 mills and 17 out of 40 pits were closed and 9,500 out of 85,000 people were unemployed.

France, the armies of Germany, France and Britain dug themselves in to long lines of opposing trenches. They settled down to a long-drawn-out and painful struggle in appalling conditions of mud and heavy bombardment, resulting in very high casualties. "Siege warfare," wrote the historian A.J.P. Taylor, "superseded decisive battles . . . . The machine gun and spade changed the course of European history."

To begin with, Britain relied on volunteers for its troops, but by 1916 so many had been killed that conscription (compulsory call-up) of men between certain ages had to be introduced. Altogether nearly three-quarters of a million of the country's younger men were killed and more than 1½ million were permanently weakened by wounds and the effects of gas.

Although farm labourers were in a "reserved occupation", as producers of vital food for the nation, many of them volunteered to join the forces. Those who remained responded successfully to the demand for increased food production and benefited from the government guarantees of higher

prices for corn and minimum wage rates for farm workers. In 1918 a vast acreage had been ploughed up and Britain was producing 80 per cent of its needs of food. But by 1929 much of the corn land had changed back to grass and British farms were only supplying 39 per cent of the country's needs of food.

After the war life was also disappointing for the workers in the towns. A "land fit for heroes" had been promised to the returning troops, but this had failed to materialize. By June 1921 unemployment had reached the 2 million mark and never went under one million between the two world wars. The areas that suffered most from foreign competition were those of the long-established heavy industries like coal-mining, iron and steel and ship-building, and traditional industries like cotton manufacturing. New industries such as the motor-car, electrical goods, chemicals and artificial fibres were doing much better. These new light industries tended to be started in the

53 Motor buses in Cowley Road, Oxford, 1914.
▼

south-east of the country, while the old industrial areas of the north, Midlands and South Wales were badly depressed.

The Age of the Motor-Car

By the outbreak of the First World War in 1914 petrol-driven cars were competing with horse-driven vehicles and the railways. Soon, motor omnibuses were replacing the horse-drawn ones in towns and there was a rapid increase in the number of private cars and lorries. Motor transport encouraged the further growth of suburbs and the separation of residential districts from industrial areas.

People no longer wanted to live within easy walking distance of their work, but could commute by bus or electric tram (as some had done before by rail), or the prosperous could come by private car.

The whole character of towns changed. The population was still growing fast: 37 million in Great Britain in 1901, 43 million by 1921 and nearly 45 million by 1931 — so, to house the increased numbers, towns spread ever outward into the new suburbs. The suburbs usually had groups of houses set back from the road and surrounded by small gardens. Many of the houses were semi-

54 Suburban street of the 1930s.
▼

detached with two or three bedrooms, two downstairs rooms and a kitchen, bathroom and inside toilet. They were much more comfortable and attractive than the old workers' houses in the town centres, which still remained as a blot on the landscape. Many of the suburban houses soon acquired a garage, as car ownership became more common. Much of the suburban housing was "ribbon development", spreading out for miles from the town into the country in narrow bands along the main roads. The suburban sprawl swallowed up many small out-lying towns and villages, which lost their identity on the edges of the large cities. In the end, some became vast built-up areas, like Greater London, Greater Manchester and Tyne and Wear, enveloping several previously separate towns and known nowadays as "conurbations".

Garden Cities

Not all town expansion was in ribbon development or monotonous housing estates. One of the pioneers in "garden suburbs" and "garden cities" was Ebenezer Howard who helped to plan and build the first Garden City at Letchworth, Hertfordshire, in 1903 and later another at Welwyn. Several garden suburbs were also built where the services of a town were combined with parks, trees and space to provide an attractive and efficient environment. The early work of pioneers in this field laid the foundations for much future town and country planning.

Working-Class Housing

One of the achievements of the Victorian period was in the end to make the towns more sanitary, though bad housing was still a serious problem. A number of private individuals such as the American, George Peabody, had given money in the 1860s to

55 A council estate of the 1930s, well-planned ➤ with individual gardens and a feeling of harmony and space.

build decent blocks of flats for working people in London. In spite of several Acts of Parliament aimed at encouraging local authorities to clear the slums and build houses, it was not until after the First World War that much progress was made. From about 1924 large council estates began to appear on the edges of the towns. Between the wars almost four million houses were built, though most of them were for private sale.

The agricultural labourer often lived in a "tied cottage" -- a house belonging to the farmer he worked for and occupied either free or at a low rent, as part of the terms of the job. The tied cottages, however, caused much ill-will, as it was felt that workers were tempted to accept lower wages in order to have a roof over their heads and they could be turned out of their homes on the whim of their employers.* Some council houses were built in the 1930s on the edges of villages for working people, while the renovated old cottages in the village centres were increasingly bought up by retired city dwellers and commuters. This put up the price of village houses and made it difficult for young people to get a home in their village. The wages of farm workers remained comparatively low, though more machinery meant that the work was less heavy and fewer men were needed. The lack of employment on the land led still more young people to move away to the towns.

Leisure Activities

During the years that followed the First World War the working week became shorter and inventions made work in the home easier for women. People had more leisure

* Tied cottages were made illegal in 1976.

52

and more opportunities to enjoy themselves. For those who could not afford a car, but wanted to get out of the town, there were coaches (charabancs) and railway excursions, cycling and the new sport of hiking. The Youth Hostel Association set up in 1929 provided cheap overnight accommodation for walkers and cyclists.

Movements like the Boy Scouts and Girl Guides and Youth Clubs associated with churches and chapels were very popular both in the towns and in the villages. The 1920s and 1930s saw more opportunity to take part in sporting activities like football, cricket, tennis and swimming, though some of these tended to be more available for the better-off. However, spectator sports, especially football, drew huge crowds of supporters. Heavy drinking by the working man had declined since 1914 — the beer was weaker, the price was higher and the licensing laws had reduced the number of public houses. The 1920s and 1930s were the heyday of the cinema, first with silent films but later with "talking pictures". Comfortable, luxuriously decorated cinemas were built in all the towns, and villagers went into the towns to see films in the evenings or at weekends. In 1937 20 million people in Britain went to the pictures each week. Evening classes to improve one's education or learn a new skill were very popular and in the country the Women's Institutes not only taught country and household crafts but provided lectures on all types of topics and numerous outings and entertainments.

Until these inter-war years holidays away from home had been the exception rather than the rule, except for the comfortably off. The Holidays with Pay Act, 1938, however, encouraged employers to give their workmen at least one week's paid holiday. Boarding houses which provided bed, breakfast and an evening meal cheaply at resorts

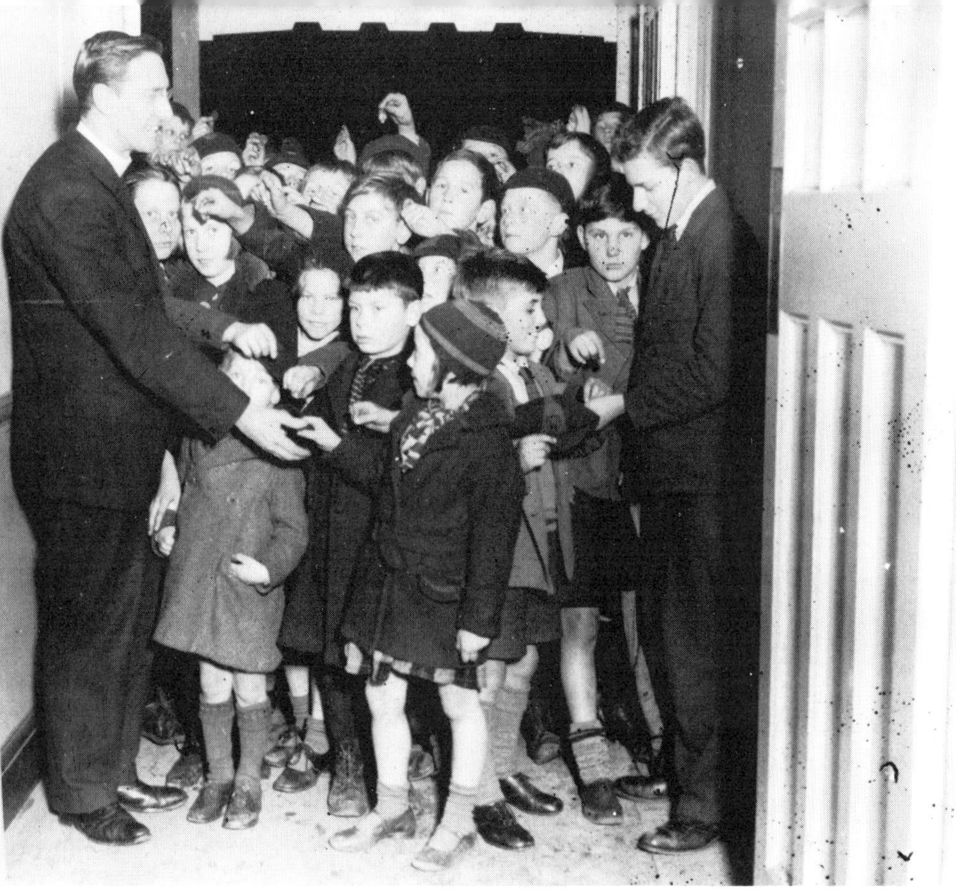

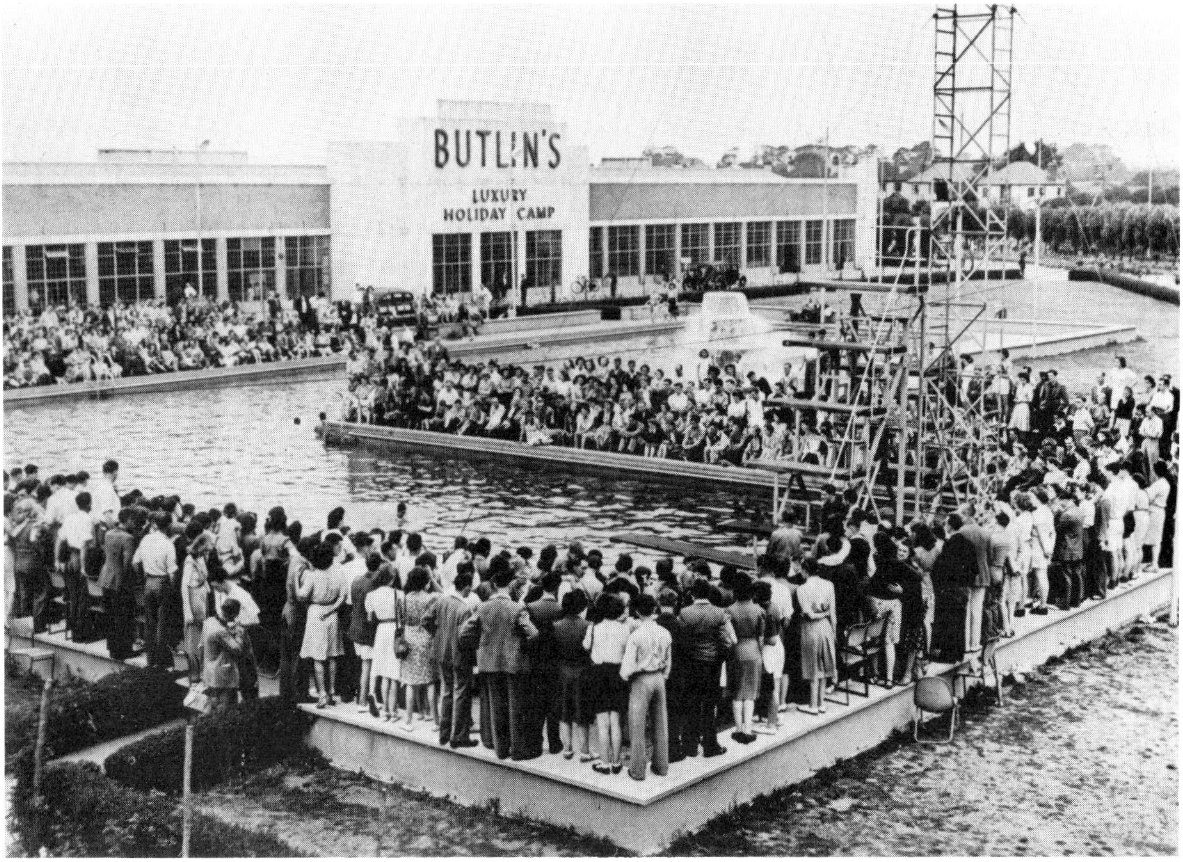
BUTLIN'S
LUXURY
HOLIDAY CAMP

56 Children crowd in to a weekly film show run by the Vicar of Welling, Kent, in 1934. They paid a penny each and the money went to the Church's work for children.

like Margate and Blackpool met some competition when Mr Billy Butlin (who opened his first camp at Skegness in 1937) and other holiday camps started to offer cheap and cheerful family holidays with fewer restrictions and more entertainment than the old-style facilities.

The Second World War and After

The Second World War was a total war, drawing on the whole resources of the nation. Unlike the First World War, when the danger was mainly restricted to young men, the 1939-1945 war, because of the role of air attack, involved the whole civilian population in risk to life.

One of the early shocks of the war occurred when the first wave of evacuation of

◄ 57 Butlin's in the 1930s.

▲
58 Children evacuated to the country from London during the Second World War.

55

schoolchildren and mothers with young babies took place from danger areas to safer country districts. The 1¼ million evacuees, mostly children, were from mainly poorer, working-class industrial and dockland districts. The countryside was suddenly confronted with the problems of urban poverty. Many of the children were in a poor physical state, infested with fleas and head lice, suffering from skin diseases and with bad habits of cleanliness and diet. This experience was to contribute to the general wish for greater social justice, for a Welfare State, after the war.

CONTRAST: Life in a "Depressed Area" and in an East Anglian Village

---

"The Town that was Murdered" — Jarrow in the 1930s

Jarrow lies near the mouth of the river Tyne on its south bank. In the days of the Venerable Bede it was a centre of European learning and the monastery there was plundered in 794 AD by the Vikings, in search of valuable church treasures. After the raid, the monks returned and their work continued there until the Dissolution of the Monasteries in 1540. Jarrow's first industries were coalmining and salt producing, but in the mid-nineteenth century a famous ship-building firm — Palmer's Shipbuilding and Iron Company — was established there. In 1821 the population of Jarrow was 3,350; fifty years later it was 18,000. Charles Palmer's shipyard prospered and he was said to have "made Jarrow", though he did not see it as in any way his duty to see that the conditions under which his workmen had to live were either sanitary or tolerable. Rows of small terrace houses were crammed together with little provision for sewage disposal and, as a result, there were frequent epidemics of typhoid and other infectious diseases.

Until the end of the First World War there was plenty of work in Jarrow and the prosperity of the shipyard seemed secure. However, by the mid-1920s countries that had previously bought their ships from Britain were now building their own. Palmer's struggled on with a thin order book until 1934, when the yard was closed down.

By June 1931, 75 per cent of the working population of the town were unemployed; a year later 80 per cent were on the dole. The writer J.B. Priestley, whose *English Journey* was, he said, "a rambling but truthful account of what one man saw and heard and felt and thought during a journey through England during the Autumn of the year 1933", visited Jarrow. He declared

Jarrow is dead . . . though as a real town . . . Jarrow can never have been alive . . . . There is no escape anywhere in Jarrow from its prevailing misery, for it is entirely a working-class town. One little street may be rather more wretched than another, but to the outsider they all look alike. One out of every two shops appeared to be permanently closed. Wherever we went there were men hanging about, not scores of them but hundreds and thousands of them . . . . The men wore the drawn masks of prisoners of war. A stranger from a distant civilisation, observing the condition of the place and its people, would have arrived at once at the conclusion that Jarrow had deeply offended some celestial emperor of the island and was now being punished. He would never believe us, if we told him that in theory this town was as good as any other and that its inhabitants were not criminals but citizens with votes.

In 1936, having sent yet another delegation to the government, asking for help for the town, the blunt answer was given that "Jarrow must work out its own solution." The local council decided to organize a march of the unemployed to London to

59   Ellen Wilkinson and local leaders at the head of the Jarrow Hunger March to London, 1936.

tell the people of England of their plight and of the treatment they had received. Miss Ellen Wilkinson, MP for Jarrow, walked with the marchers and recorded their story in her book, *The Town That Was Murdered*. The march was officially organized by the Town Council and requests for overnight accommodation and facilities in church halls or other premises were signed by the mayor. A large number of men volunteered to go, but the number accepted was limited to 200, who had to pass a medical examination.

The marchers took two petitions to the House of Commons, one signed by the citizens of Jarrow and the second from the towns of Tyneside, arriving for the opening of a new session of Parliament. A public meeting was held where they stopped each night, though it was aimed to keep the protests non-party political. Most of the marchers were in shabby caps and suits with mackintosh capes, but at the head was Councillor Riley in a lounge suit and bowler and the tiny, smart red-haired MP, Ellen Wilkinson.

The men had an improvised mouth organ band to help them keep reasonably in step.

Although some days when it poured with rain were lowering, most of the men enjoyed the hard slog — they had devoted medical attention from volunteer medical students; they had three meals a day and, as one of them said, he woke knowing he had "something worthwhile to do". They appreciated the sympathy and hospitality (meals, municipal hot baths at Barnsley and the Cooperative Society boot repair shop at Leicester which stayed open all night to repair their boots free).

They arrived at the Houses of Parliament soaked to the skin, "the picture of a walking distressed area" and handed in their two petitions. No one expected a miracle and none occurred, though a new steel mill was later set up on the site of Palmer's shipyard. However, the Jarrow Crusade stirred the conscience of the nation and has gone into the history books.

Some Recollections of the 1930s in the Village of "Akenfield"

To write his portrait of the East Anglian village of Akenfield (not its real name) in the 1960s, Ronald Blythe tape-recorded the reminiscences of old people who had lived there all, or most of their lives, as well as the views of younger people and more recent incomers. The book has provided a unique history of a village by the villagers in their own words. Mr Blythe has, of course, unobtrusively researched the background, managed to get the characters themselves to dredge up their recollections and give him their confidences, and knitted the whole material together to produce a valuable social document.

Although Ronald Blythe has been very successful in getting some Akenfield people to talk about the old days, he found them essentially "private folk" and not inclined to gossip. "The old ones have emerged from indignities and sufferings," he writes, "which taught a man to hold his tongue." Several villagers commented on this aspect of their lives. "It took a brave man to show his politics in Suffolk all through the 1930s," said 71-year-old Leonard Thompson, "if you weren't a Tory you were a trouble-maker." 85-year-old Fred Mitchell made the same point:

You had nearly to perish to bring up a family then. . . . There wasn't a penny for nothing. . . . I never had no good times. I had to accept everything my governor said to me. I learnt never to answer a word. I dursn't say nothing. Today you can be a man with men, but not then. . . . I lived when other men could do what they liked with me. We feared so much. We even feared the weather! [They got no pay if they were sent home.] *We dreaded the rain; it washed out our few shillings.*

Even the independent craftsmen like Jubal Merton, a wheelwright, said: "No man dare open his mouth, or out he went! A man had to be silent to stay in the village." One of the reasons why the labourers dared not answer back was the fear that the farmer would turn them and their families out of their "tied cottages".

The old labourers also commented on the hardness of the work they did and their low pay. Leonard Thompson recalled that after he joined the army in 1914, during his first four months' training with the regiment, he put on nearly a stone in weight and got a bit taller. It was not just more food but

for the first time in my life there had been no strenuous work. I want to say this simply as a fact, that village people in Suffolk in my day were worked to death. It literally happened. It is not a figure of speech. I was worked mercilessly. I am not complaining about it. It is what happened to me.

"The farmer had got the upper hand," said Jubal Merton

and wherever he could he made his work-er his slave. . . . The farmers had become too powerful — and mean! It wasn't their talk that separated them from the gentry, it was their meanness.

Thatcher Ernie Bowers, an independent craftsman, said he was glad he never worked as a farm labourer:

The farmers round here treated their men shameful before the war and none of us forgets this.

Looking back on the 1930s, few of the villagers had much in the way of pleasures to remember, but they did seem to miss the simple experiences of conversation, joking and singing songs. Jubal Merton, the wheel-wright, commented that what he had noticed most about the village was "the way people no longer want to get together. It was a regular thing for twenty or more folk to sit on that bank outside the shop and talk of an evening." Fred Mitchell, now disabled and in a wheelchair, watched the boys playing football and riding their bikes. "I never did any playing in all my life," he said. "There was nothing in my childhood, only work. I never had any pleasure." Then he remembered something and said he had forgotten "the singing". "The Chapels were full of singing . . . so I lie; I have had pleasure. I have had singing."

60   Durham, 1930s: a group of workers on a bogie, having a break during hay-time.
▼

6
After the War and into the 1980s

Post-War Building and Town Planning

61 Many of the post-war housing estates were stark concrete blocks like the L.C.C.'s Minerva Street estate, Bethnal Green, which contained 261 flats.

▼

When the war in Europe was over in 1945 and a new government was elected in Britain, one of the first problems to confront it

was a serious shortage of houses. There had been no building for several years; more than 200,000 houses had been destroyed, 250,000 badly damaged and over 4 million partly damaged by enemy bombing. Thousands of schools, churches, shops, factories and other buildings had also been destroyed or damaged. To make matters worse, there was an acute shortage of building materials, especially wood. The government restricted the amount of private building and embarked on a programme of subsidized house building by local authorities; in four years 800,000 houses were built.

During the war a Royal Commission had considered ways of improving conditions in the towns and, as a result of its proposals (in the Barlow Report, 1940), the Town and Country Planning Act (1947) gave the government powers to control new building. Enemy bombing had laid waste some city centres and destroyed much slum property, which gave the opportunity to rebuild parts of towns. Under the direction of, and with grants from, the new Ministry of Town and Country Planning, (later called the Ministry of Housing and Local Government), new roads, schools, hospitals, factories and houses, well-planned to improve working and living conditions, sprang up all over the country. Between 1950 and 1955 nearly 1½ million council houses were built in England and Wales. By 1956 a quarter of the population lived in publicly-owned housing. Major rehousing schemes provided new estates on the outskirts of towns and in inner-city areas.

To relieve some of the congestion in industrial areas, the government built some completely new towns. Under the New Towns Act of 1946, fourteen self-contained towns were built, with their own industries, schools, shopping and community centres and houses laid out in pleasant surroundings. Crawley, Harlow and Hatfield were among the early New Towns and more recently the idea has been copied at places like Milton Keynes in Buckinghamshire and

Washington on Tyneside. The principles of design of these new towns were revolutionary. Through-traffic was kept at the edge of the towns, and residential and communal areas were kept separate from industry. Although some social problems have been caused by uprooting city people and putting them down in a new environment at a distance from their families and friends, on the whole, families have benefited from quieter, safer and healthier lives, with employment near at hand.

As well as providing more homes, the various post-war governments have felt responsible for preventing the continual spread of towns into the countryside. The "Green Belt" policy has given protection against any further building in a belt, or ring, perhaps 8 kilometres wide, around large towns. The green belts help to preserve the countryside for town dwellers to get out into and protect good agricultural land from being swallowed up by industry.

Nevertheless, with the population continuing to increase (nearly 56 million in the United Kingdom in 1980), the problems of overcrowding and of the countryside shrinking, as a result of development schemes, remain serious. Towns have grown upwards as well as outwards, so that the sky-lines of our cities are now dominated by sky-scrapers and not by church spires and cathedrals. Many towns have built tower blocks of flats, but there has been a strong reaction against these high-rise dwellings where some people feel isolated and unhappy and which have proved to be unsatisfactory for families with small children. Moreover, some of these blocks have been found to be structurally unsound and have had to be demolished.

The Traffic Problem

Congestion of motor vehicles in towns is no less of a problem than the overcrowding of people. From the 1950s onwards there has been a rapid increase in the number of private

▲
62　Cumbernauld New Town is pleasantly land-scaped with trees and pedestrian areas, with through traffic excluded, making it safe for children and quiet for adults.

cars, and by 1979 about 58 per cent of all households in Great Britain owned a car and 13 per cent had two or more cars. Traffic jams block the streets in towns and the air is polluted with exhaust fumes. The motorist finds the hold-ups frustrating and it is diffi-cult to park his or her car. Multi-storey and underground car parks, as well as urban clearways to keep the traffic moving and space rationing by parking meters or other systems, have been provided in many towns. But recently it has been argued that extra parking space attracts extra traffic and maybe cars should be banned from town centres. Motorists would then have to park their cars at the edge of towns and continue their journeys on public transport. To offset the domination of the car in towns, pedestrian precincts have been made, where vehicles are excluded and people can shop in safety and away from the noise and smell of traffic.

Cars, however, are only part of the problem. In the 1960s many unprofitable local railway lines were closed down under the Beeching Plan (1963) and British Rail concentrated on busy commuter traffic, fast inter-city routes and long-distance freight services. Nearly half the railway mileage of 1918 was lost. As a result, ever more lorries and vans, and recently the massive "juggernauts", were putting enormous strains on Britain's out-of-date system of roads. The building of a network of motorways was embarked on in the 1960s, designed for fast

long-distance traffic. By-passes have been made around many towns and villages, to prevent them being swamped by heavy through-traffic.

Change in the Villages

These radical developments in transport have brought great changes to village life. The stream of incomers commuting to the towns for their work, which was noted earlier, halted the decay of villages caused by villagers moving to the towns. Since the nineteenth century there has been a steady decline in the number of people employed on the land. By the end of the 1970s only 2.7 per cent of the British population was employed in agriculture, although 73 per cent of the land surface was still in agricultural use. Farming has become a highly

63   Congestion of the old A2 London to Dover road near Canterbury before the by-pass was built.
▼

▲
64   Cars from the village of Eynsham join the
stream of traffic to the town.

65   Villages like Combe in Oxfordshire which have ▶
lost their shops are now served by enormous
grocery vans once a week.

efficient, mechanized industry and farms
employ few local inhabitants. Farms have
become fewer, larger and more specialized;
they are often combined into large units, run
by a manager, but even smaller farms are run
by a farmer with perhaps one helper from
his family. The village craftsman, too, has all
but disappeared from the countryside, so
that the opportunities for employment in
the villages are almost non-existent, apart
from a little work connected with tourism or
recreational facilities. The native villager,
like the newcomers, must commute to the
towns for his work.

66 Protest by parents and children at the proposed ►
closure of the village school at Madingley, Cambridge-
shire in 1978. One of the banners read "Keep the
Heart of our Community".

Up to the Second World War, while the villages were shrinking in size, most of the village institutions like the church, chapel, a school, a post office and several shops as well as a blacksmith and builder still existed. Oddly enough, now, although the villages have grown and are flourishing, the number of services has declined. Because so many villagers now have a motor car, people shop at the cheaper supermarkets in the towns, and the local stores cannot keep going. Many villages are now without a shop or post office, and bus services which no longer pay are reduced or withdrawn. The old, the young and the less well-off suffer most from the isolation and lack of services. Many village schools have been closed because of falling rolls and so the children are taken by school bus to the town or another village. The loss of the school in a village is loss of part of the community life, as is the closing of parish churches which is happening at the rate of about one hundred a year in England.

As the motorways make a quick escape to the country easier, competition for desirable village houses has often pushed up prices far beyond the reach of the native villagers. Sometimes the houses are bought as week-end retreats or holiday homes, and this can cause local hostility. The villager without a rented cottage or a council house may have to move to the town.

While some of the newcomers are only occasional residents, most of them tend to be enthusiastic supporters of village societies and conservation groups. Dramatic societies, cricket teams and Women's Institutes flourish and the villages are often kept much neater and in better order than in the past. The new villagers are quick and active if they feel their quiet village is in any danger from, say, a new motorway or airport.

Town Centre Decay

As a result of traffic congestion in the towns and bad planning which allowed working-class homes and industry to grow side by side, many town centres are not pleasant places in which to live. Since rents and rates are high there, and transport costs are rising, many firms have moved out of the towns into the suburbs or country towns and some city centres have fallen into decay. There is less employment in the town centres, but there are still many people who have nowhere else to live except in these run-down, unattractive districts. This applies particularly to Commonwealth immigrants who have settled in such areas through lack of money and also the tendency to be near people of their own ethnic group. Concentrations of people from the West Indies in districts of London like Brixton or from Pakistan in Southall have led to racial prejudice and tension. Violence and delinquency have also increased in urban areas, partly as a result of the frustration felt by some young people living in high-rise flats and dreary housing estates without facilities for communal entertainment. Since the late 1970s serious and increasing unemployment and cuts in local authority services have inevitably made these social problems worse.

67 Traditional May Day celebrations in the village of Combe, Oxfordshire.
▼

Sudbourne in Suffolk in the late 1970s*

Sudbourne no longer has a shop or post office. It has no school, its hospital has closed down and its bus service is sparse, inconvenient and expensive. Those who have no private cars are increasingly isolated. An article by Philip Norman in 1978 makes the point that, as a result of thirty years of social change, the old, the poor, the unemployed and the sick and disabled have been stranded in the villages and that there is public indifference to their plight:

There was a different village here. It exists now only in clues . . . . School Road, Hospital Road, lead one blandly, each to a cul-de-sac of distance and forest edge. The school has become a private house, its Gothic class-room windows shortened . . . sold to a barrister from London. . . . There was once a shop, they say, at Red House. Its vanished windows haunt it still in the shape of paler bricks. Inside the telephone kiosk a plaque informs the user he is speaking from 'Sudbourne Post Office and Stores.' Looking out, he sees a white housefront, a new double garage, a pale blue, exclusive looking door. The Post Office shut down three years ago . . .

For all practicable purposes Sudbourne depends on local authority transport, that modern form of charity. School buses take its children to Orford, Butley or Woodbridge. A mobile library calls on alternate Fridays, staying half an hour. Once a fortnight, a County Council minibus takes the elderly to Orford, to collect their pensions and enjoy half an hour's shopping in the metropolitan at-

* From an article "Is There Life After Death" by Philip Norman in the *Sunday Times Weekly Review*, 29th January 1978.

mosphere of a Post Office, a sweetshop and Elliott's general store. Not even this conveyance has been able to deliver 83 year old Mrs. Daisy Knights to her house a quarter of a mile from Corner Farm.

Mr Norman's article is entitled "Is There Life After Death?". He clearly thinks there is little life for old people in "dead" villages like Sudbourne:

In Sudbourne, or any lonely village, passing some retired couple's bungalow, one can almost envy them . . . round a warm blue television screen. Old people, no less than young, seem wonderfully adaptable. . . . When their local shops close down they simply go without, when their buses are withdrawn, they somehow struggle on. The world in their eyes is growing madder . . . more dangerous, yet they persistently keep alive, forming . . . no pressure groups, not complaining, only grumbling in voices they do not expect to be heeded.

Trouble in Toxteth, July 1981

The name Toxteth hit the world headlines in July 1981. Toxteth is in inner Liverpool, a once-great port which for various reasons has greatly declined. 60 per cent of local blacks live in Toxteth, which is an area of exceptionally high unemployment. 60 per cent more young blacks are unemployed than young whites. Housing is another serious problem in this decayed town-centre district. While similar proportions of black and white tenants applied to be rehoused outside the inner area, whites were almost three times as likely to succeed than blacks. Partly because of cut-backs in local authority spending, little had been done recently in this district to try to meet the special needs of the black community nor to attempt to solve the problem of race relations. It is not surprising that all this created an explosive mixture which led to rioting and clashes between black and white youths and the police.

Toxteth was not, of course, the first. Three months of street clashes and looting in different parts of the country had had a snowball effect. The common factor was discontent among the young people living in inner urban areas of high unemployment and resentment towards authority, especially the police.

The dramatic rioting in London, Liverpool and other cities has certainly highlighted the problems of inner-city life. A swift response from the government promises a more effective Youth Opportunities Programme and more extensive Training Schemes. Housing, social services, including amenities for young people, relations with the police and education are also areas where improvement is needed. It remains to be seen whether these first-aid measures can be effective against such deep-rooted problems.

Smoothing Out the Differences

Throughout this book we have been comparing life in the village with life in the town at various points in history, but there is no doubt that recent developments such as the ever-present motor-car and the television set have blurred the differences. The isolation of the country-dweller from the bright lights of the town has largely disappeared except for the old and the poor. The ignorance of the town-dweller about the countryside has largely disappeared, except for the "disadvantaged" groups in the community. The numbers who live in remote country districts are very few and those who live in town centres are steadily decreasing. Most of us live between country and town in the suburbs. The sharp contrasts between the life styles of town and country have largely gone.

68 After the riots in Toxteth, Liverpool, July 1981.
▼

Books for Further Reading

There are a large number of books in this field from which those listed below are recommended as examples. Some (marked with a *) are rather difficult and detailed but are suggested as books to dip into and because they have interesting illustrations.

A. Allen,
The Story of the Village,
Faber

E. Boog-Watson and J.I. Carruthers,
Country Life Through the Ages,
Allen and Unwin

T.K. Butcher,
Country Life,
Batsford, 1970

*John S. Creasey,
*Victorian and Edwardian Country Life
from old photographs*,
Batsford, 1977

*George Ewart Evans,
The Farm and the Village,
Faber, 1974

*G. Fielden Hughes,
Looking Back at Rural Life,
E.P. Publishing Ltd, 1975

Peter Moss,
Town Life Through the Ages,
Harrap, 1972

*R. Muir,
The English Village,
Thames and Hudson, 1980

M. and C.H.B. Quennell,
A History of Everyday Things in England
series,
Batsford

M.E. Reeves,
The Medieval Town,
Longman ("Then and There" series)

M.E. Reeves,
The Medieval Village,
Longman ("Then and There" series)

*A. Ridley,
Living in Cities,
Heinemann, 1971

*Robert Trow-Smith,
Farming Through the Ages in Pictures,
Farming Press Ltd, 1978

*Colin Ward,
The Child in the City,
The Architectural Press Ltd, 1978

Charles Whynne-Hammond,
Towns,
Batsford, 1976

_____ Places to Visit _____

A large number of museums and historical houses open to the public have on show exhibits such as furnished rooms and farming or industrial equipment through the ages. It is impossible to list them all, but if you wish to discover whether there is a suitable museum or historic house near your home or where you are going on holiday, you should consult _Museums and Galleries in Great Britain and Ireland_, published each year by ABC Historic Publications, which you should be able to find in the reference section of your local library.

Here are a few examples of museums with interesting collections in this field:

Acton Scott Working Farm Museum,
    Wenlock Lodge, Acton Scott,
    near Church Stretton, Salop

Ardress (N. Ireland) Agricultural Museum,
    County Armagh

Aston Munslow Whitehouse Museum of
    Buildings and Country Life, Salop

Beamish, Co. Durham, North of England
    Open Air Museum, near Chester-le-Street

Black Country Museum, Tipton Road,
    Dudley, West Midlands

Cambridge and County Folk Museum,
    2 and 3 Castle Street, Cambridge

Gressenhall (Norfolk), Norfolk Rural Life
    Museum, Beech House, Gressenhall,
    Dereham, NR20 4DR

Hawes (N. Yorks), Upper Dales Folk Museum,
    Station Yard, Hawes

Leicester, Newarke Houses Museum

London, the Museum of London,
    London Wall, EC2

Norwich, Strangers Hall, Charing Cross

Reading (Berks), Museum of Rural Life,
    White Knights Park, University of Reading

Telford, Ironbridge Gorge Museum, Salop

Witney (Oxfordshire), Manor Farm Museum,
    Cogges, Near Witney

York, Castle Museum, Tower Street, York

Index

The numbers in **bold type** refer to the figure numbers of the illustrations

71

72